Reading TUB BUNNY makes one glad to be alive! Basinski is an intimate philosopher, ever sardonic, pondering: "Her ghost said: you know who I am, I know you know who I am, I know you know I am you." Sublime subconscious mind. *Tub Bunny* whets us from the very first with playful, pun-full sonority: "Flapping his gums wildly, his wild ghost wildly said: wild and sweet, pure white crabapple blossoms . . . Shelley rhymes with her belly." This is the kind of sonorous poetry that inspires in this realm and the next; the kind that lives in the mind way beyond the song's strumming.

    Heather Woods, author of *Light Bearing*

Self described as "a syndicate of types" *Tub Bunny* is that and more. It is a breaking of types, of poetry presumptions, of the pretense of projective dictums, of pre-determined language assumptions & LANGUAGE school restrictions. This is verse truly free. It has its predecessors : Rimbaud's "Vowels", e e cummings' language playground, Vachel Lindsay's "aural and temporal experience", Kenneth Patchen's "Orange Bears" and, AND, *Albion Moonlight*, Keroauc's "broken eggs" of wasted words, and most of all Velimir Khlebnikov's *Zangezi* (but also his poems of the Russian Civil War that rivaled the Objectivists' precise present of historical fact). *Tub Bunny*, a book, a real book, of wonder and delight.
    Joe Napora

Michael Basinski's *Tub Bunny* is full of "Impure vowels. / Hypnotic spellings." Poetry haunts his and her ghosts. They sing about Cheektowaga, NY, USA, where winter haunts the Walden fields of May, June, and July. The summer months of Buffalo—"lawn fates," carnival games, Iroquois draft for $1 a large cup! Imagine that! The consumption of teenage lust (how it's never enough), like John Keats surviving off anchovies and a single loaf (Al Cohen's seeded rye?). The diet was intended to reduce blood flow to his stomach. Basinski writes, "Such is his nature of his being haunted. He could see things in the dark, and he was tongue tied." Say the dark is history. Say it's the past. Some would say the dark's old desires, old memories. I say it's a movie half-remembered projected on the silver screen, ghosts silently watching. Michael Basinski's *Tub Bunny* provides a light for this darkness that surrounds us. Or is it a laff in the dark?
    Patrick Riedy

***Tub Bunny* is an insatiable mind treat**, an apparitional masterpiece. It revels in place and history (mostly Buffalo and surrounding areas) and the ghosts still alive there—hanging out, commenting and haunting both. With the ghosts, I sang along, participated, succumbed to belly gut laughter, got lost/found and challenged as leaping associations proliferated and multiple forms of text unfolded. The ghosts of Olson, Duncan and Blevins (alive and well) drifted in and out of my mind during the poetic roller coaster ride. Basinki's encyclopedic talent astonishes – a creative talent that offers a poetry profoundly awake and fresh, shaking language from its doldrums into its possibilities. My ghost said: "What a wild ride!"
    Richard Martin

Tub Bunny

Michael Basinski

Spuyten Duyvil
New York City

Some form of these apparitions first appeared in *New American Writing, Volt, Dispatches from the Poetry Wars, Fell Swoop,* and *Peach Mag,* and in the form of an electronic chapbook: *Ghosts of June Ghost Syndical* in *Dispatches from the Poetry Wars.*

© 2020 Michael Basinski
ISBN 978-1-952419-00-3
Cover art: Michael Basinski

Library of Congress Cataloging-in-Publication Data

Names: Basinski, Michael, author.
Title: Tub bunny / Michael Basinski.
Description: New York City : Spuyten Duyvil, [2020] |
Identifiers: LCCN 2020018622 | ISBN 9781952419003 (paperback)
Subjects: LCGFT: Poetry.
Classification: LCC PS3552.A8133 T83 2020 | DDC 811/.54--dc23
LC record available at https://lccn.loc.gov/2020018622

For the Djinn

Tub Bunny could be an expansive paratactic form, shaped with bathos, with trajectories, made with meander, whimsey, a syndicate of all types, all categories of poetry enjambed and juxtaposed, exposed, and eroded, and fused with sarcasm and eros, humor, and the absurd, and narration, performance text, popular song, fact, magic, myth, and the supernatural, and with confession, and with confusion, and *Tub Bunny* congregates compositional curves and swerves, and in particular *Tub Bunny* is time collage that is any mid-June, July, and the week beyond the beginning of Lammas.

I could hear the ghostly gentle June
bellow of the warm solstice breeze
through the leaves
of the eastern cottonwoods
Yooooooooo!, Yooooooooo!, Yooooooooo!, tub bunny.

Johnny Wadsworth Longfellow

Praeludium

While driving on George Urban Boulevard by Queen of Martyrs in Cheektowaga, a man with an alleged .07 percent alcohol level had an accident, and his car was on a person's front lawn. Marijuana and a burnt marijuana cigarette were reportedly in the vehicle. When asked to recite the alphabet from C to R the man said: H, M, L, H, R.

SING

(with a form of solemnity)

V and W
U E Z
G
L X
D T
C H O
P N E
J A
I
B Q
K R
Y
S M

Open Containers

Her ghost said: I am all that hath been, and is, and shall be, and my veil no mortal has hitherto raised.
Ghost incantāre: Chic-key-two-a-gua, Ji-ik-do-wah-gah, Chictawauga, Cheektowaga: land of the wild crabapple in the Seneca tongue.
Flapping his gums wildly, his wild ghost wildly said: wild and sweet, pure white crabapple blossoms are wildly perfume sweet, and Callery pear blossoms smell weird, smells like StarKist in here, the wooden temple of the Walden moon, open on Walden Avenue, at sun sat, for business, Shelley rhymes with her belly.
From a radio, playing distantly:
♪ Shelly brand meat products
♪ Really grand meat products
♪ Old fashion good
♪ by Szelagowski.
During Mass at Queen of Martyrs, the Holy Ghost appears, above her hands folded in prayer, while she thinks about, necking.
Her ghost was the genus Malus, the thorny red rose family, Rosaceae.
Thorns of wild crabapple can be two inches long and sharp, and prick.
According to the canonical Gospels a woven ring of thorns was placed upon the head of Jesus on his Way of Grief.
The ring of red thorns was one of the musical instruments of the Passion.
A multicolor and musical Crown of Thorns can be purchased at Walmart for $14.95.
The fruit is a globose pome a pome, derived from Latin *pōmum*, meaning fruit touched him in the dark.
His ghost said: I swear I, saw, her shadow moved.
During the May rite of farewell, she pricked wildly at the white flower blossoms of her wildflower crown, CYO.
Pin prick infections are common among those that love, roses.
Crushed rose petal beads were sanctioned by the Catholic Church for rosaries as far back as the 16th century.
A copped crabapple is the size of a cherry.
Rose touched the spinning wheel's spindle prick.
Five-finger discount is a popular term used for theft.
The early empty bird catches the worm in the Walden fields, New York

Central Railroad train-track, empty boxcars, smell the empty odor of boy, fantasy, a buzzing fly, sawdust, termites, carpenter ants, crabapples.
Denny the Pope's ghost said: I caught the crabs again, someplace, a doorknob. Someplace.
Mark's ghost said: call me crabs.
Crabbed handwriting is weird, ill-formed, and hard to figure out.
There were eleven wild swans by a pile of rotting railroad ties, slivers waiting in waiting.
His ghost said emphatically: I've begged you until I'm blue in the face, blushed.
Her ghost said: you must have dog shit in your ears, clean-em out, like,, a empty gondola car.
A white swan nibbled in his ear like you do on any other living thing but much gentler.
His ghost said: all my life my small wishes have fallen, dead, as crows, or flies, as the, out of the sky, onto deaf ears, a pile of burning leaves, and were lost in the shuffle of cards, wings, Hitchcock's *The Birds*.
Her ghost said: I looked under the couch already but I musta loozed it, tough shit, no love lost.
Tapinoma melanocephalum is a type of ant commonly called the ghost ant, dark head, and pale or translucent legs and gaster.
Her ghost said: I kinda feel like I got ants in the pants.
She was no Queen of Sheba.
His ghost said: I mind as well be talkin to myself, what's on my mind, I never listen, won't hear what's good for me, I guess, stupid.
In the Walden fields, he heard something sweet, a black ant high, and frantic among the crabapple thorns in one of the hundreds of crabapple trees, in every crabapple tree, ever, over, where someone dragged a mattress, you know what for.

h

that time forgot

Neisner's five-and-dime at the Thruway Plaza, Cheektowaga, where
the lush lust lunch counter curves of plates, front, red covered counter
stools, spin by the biggest plate glass big windows, and the photobooth,
misty gumball machine, a waitress asked: what can I give you?
His ghost said: BLT.
Her ghost said: Opener of the Ways, Weaver of Water, eggshells, eggshell,
I am Beltane May, in time to smell his ghost swell in your milky thin
crick water, cloudy, wovenings, make-a-date, blind date, sell-by-date,
Saturday, afternoon.
♪ I will give you caps of blue and silver sunlight for your hair
♪ All that soon will be is what you need to see.
Out of focus, fuzzy, it's coming back to me in bits, and pieces.

Incantation: some, time in June, dressed as a witch, a spider, a spear
pierced his side and poured out forthwith came there out her blood
waves and curls, and my curves and whey, and water curls in June
1937, Cayuga Creek overflowed with a maximum discharge of 18,000
ft^3 per second flooded freely in waves flows down her throat dark and
flammable his greasy heart soaking her adoration, head to toe, soaking
wet, her flames soaked by his stinking fire engine hose, how can I love
you when I soaked you, immerse in my perfumed playground darkness
deep and wicked guilt and grief and candle heat and burning the drug
frankincense rescues the experience of spiritual beings, let me count the
ways, his monster was homemade, hers flush.

Experiencing huge fluctuations in temperature, French fries.
In the photobooth she passion bit him, a P.B., her swift water her running
fast, cold and high with hazards, and we swam swift water maneuvering
her in the forest green Buick.
He said: BLT, white bread.
♪ Dem bones, dem bones gonna walk around.

After, she spelt: waiting to get on the NFT Sycamore 6 bus to go downtown on the side of Neisner's, for free, Saturday, he could not sleep, often forgetful open as he was waist deep in her open water up to his balls scrotum their waves washed away her debris on his beach, wash away his regret and her sins of the world was her springing eternal summer, broken spring in his couch and broken spring in his white and black prefrontal cortex, fed out a strip of black and white photographs appeared haunted from the side of his old photobooth hippocampus, figures dance a round dance bedside her bonfire a round dance wear nothing on the bus Beltane, on fire, is yellow and blush red brushed by him a ghost always sat next to him, holding his hand, while she vomited flowers out, the white and red NFT bus, bus window.

b Preluding

Beaver Island Beach is not on Beaver Island. Beaver Island, yes, there is such a place! Imagine! Say three Hail Marys.
Nit, Net, an ancient goddess of weaving before the deluge the Thruway Plaza in Cheektowaga opened in 1952. Think Memphis, think Ptah, Ptah created ghosts through the power of his own heart and his own speech. There were 47 great stores, including Grants, Neisner's, L.L. Berger, Cavages. The Cisco Kid signed autographs on opening day. Jaryło, lost. Where the grave of Osiris was located? I don't know? Idonotgetit? And that his sufferings were displayed as a mystery of night. Neith the goddess of Sais, of war, due to the extensive destruction by peasants removing mud brick time deposits for use as fertilizer leaving only a few relief blocks appear to be what remains are wispy forms of sand turned into glass circles in intense heat and translucent absolutions float on the creek water randomly at midsummer, which once belonged to her and would reappear in its usual spot, sometimes when she reached into his pocket for his Pontiac car keys.

b

Picnic Songs of the Young, Sweet, and Stupid

The seventeenth episode of *The Prisoner* aired in 1968. Titled: *Fall Out*, the issue featured "All You Need Is Love" by The Beatles. It was the only time ever a Beatles song was licensed to a TV show.
♪ How to be you in time. It's easy.

Incantations have often been sung in strange constellations when the ghost's heart is being weighted by Anubis.
An Anubis incant: he could be forgetful see the brick bottom the masonry mystery by night a wide-mouthed Mason glass jar with an airtight screw-top offering snails, Stations of the Cross, and Easter red algae with his tongue flat as a table salt licked the lid dreaming of her tiny tits.

An Anubis incant: I needed her Baby Doll bathing suit quick-drying and perfect for women on the move, make, down his unblended river of blemishes as the sun roses dreaming of two eggs sunny-side up.
His ghost said: I've had too much sun, I'm burned.
Her ghost incanted: to bite him Neith she licked her lips, chap stick lip butter draped bruises night a red-blue color, biliverdin producing a green color, bilirubin producing a yellow color, and hemosiderin producing a golden-brown color marked clouds on his neck, a lace meandering cloudy at tonight clotted her hot rollers make beautiful barrel waves ornament moon organs of Late Latin blundus yellow.

An Anubis incant: in prayer passion boggles his mouth full of rosary beads of poppy seeds of sweat and quicksand that he licked what spoon she left after he frosted Communion.
I lost my balance in his broken veins and dropping bruised her moist mucus most incubus cupcakes and sugars of grace bleached flour in St. Sloppy Joe's emergency room hospital on Harlem Road to pump his stomach he dreaming of her.

His ghost said: I in my thorn woods would wait, wait in the Confession line at St. John Gualbert's and prepare my false sins my false sins wait untrue.
Her ghost said: I am the city of red roses and my crown of thorns, a ring of my animal horns clarinet, for you, you're the only one I can do this with.

An Anubis incant: in his knee deep velvet deep lashed red of blood carpet polished cherry, maple, and oak and marble Stations of the Passion on the tip of the island his taken up by the ruins of the Temple of Khnum Abu or Yebu or Elephantine Satis, Satet, Satjit, Sates, Sati, I worship when seen she his bountiful annual flood of the Nile.

An Anubis incant: Luxor wash clothed his sponge bath she hoped to wash her guilt away in Confession confusing to all of her forgiveness to his sins of the world her Catholic glutton licked gluten gives elasticity to dough, electricity helps it rise and keeps its shape and often she gives the final product the chewy texture to his alphabet, bather, cherry butter.

Her ghost said to him: a huge collection of Linen Bath Towels. Bliss Egyptian Cotton Luxury Towels, at Luxor Linens, we like taking that sensation of relaxation further, at J. C. Penney's, piles of towels, beach towels of endless cobalt blue and to protect her identity from ghosts the green towel of her eyes were my breakfast every goddess spelt without vowels, hidden ink somewhere in his dark, tangled, rite.

Her ghost said: abracadabra, unhook my abracadabra, Bailey show afternoon Sunday, by this way I protect you from witches and keep you all for myself, yummm.

c

1968, Roman Polanski, after moving into a Manhattan apartment with her husband the teenage Rosemary Woodhouse begins to experience odd, unpleasant things, abnormal, poetry, random, bizarre, to be breathing still, still, always, seated, dark, flickering, adjusting to seat, see in the secret.
Pete's ghost said: I know this guy slipped his dick into the bottom of a buttered popcorn box so his girlfriend when she reached in for popcorn, no lie.

The lights switching on and off, click-clack, click-clack, in between his ghost said: I am the ruins of the ram god of Elephantine, some pie smear of pie on a blueberry pie plate whether you're dealing with butter or marriage margarine stains or other great greasy kitchen stains, Tide can help her clean up a grease stain she could not be lifted.

Her broom became tangled in her long thin summer skirt and she charmed, red fire hydrants, he could only imagine her nipples sitting next to her in the Center Theatre in downtown Buffalo, outside was a line Main Street waiting to get in, reserved seating, he completely undresses her until she shivers and naked, and fingers at him abruptly seen wearing a floral bathing suit on the Sistine Chapel ceiling, her typhoon at sea, and his naked descent into the hold of a sunken ship, in Lake Erie, held her where a bonfire burns, and Rosemary lies on a Perfect Sleeper mattress.

Her ghost charmed him: June will always lie to you and you will yearn to eat her sins at the scene of the crime, contaminated corporal punishment, Cupid culprit. Signed Chalk Fairy.

I will accept your offering, he could do nothing but listen and obey, and I can only make you wish, blow out the candles.

His ghost said: I offer the feeble trickle flowing from the faucet of my heart.

In her dreamlike sleep, he changes into a grotesque beastlike alphabet figures resembling her hemlock wish and wild horse chestnut, with yellowish eyes and with his carrot fingers he believed in arson.

The lights switching on and off, her ghost enchanted: he has eyes lashed my June mast Mass undulations of this underwater world awaits you, felon, wait in line, never moves.

The lights switching on and off, her ghost said: you can only eat potato pancakes or fish on Friday, and far more insidious, dangerous, and invisible then him her are those who retreat into a place either deep inside himselves or flee to a place outside of her bodies.

June just like I did as children during the times of their assault when the nun took him to the front of the room and beat him with which her thick yard stick from Zolte's lumber.

The week before Palm Sunday, she remembered, preparing the palms, stripping away the bent leaves, the dry leaves, I found palm worms in the cut palms among the palm leaves and between my devotions crushed them.

Christopher held a palm worm on his open palm ticklish he folded his hands to whistle the Hail Mary.

The Palace Burlesk was the crown jewel of Shelton Square. Both the Palace and Shelton Square were wiped off the map in the late 1960s, when the tightly packed, tangle of century-old buildings were wiped out for the Main Place Tower and the M&T Building. Ostara. Birthplace of Hathor since demolished. St Joseph's Cathedral was gifted major repairs to the north and south transepts in 1924 and the towers were removed in 1927. The exterior marble started to separate from the brick, opening. Between March 31 and April 6, 1967, a tempest swirl as an old Erie cold spring wind witch she sheers the demolition was complete. The lights went off and she cast with her confused fingers. After that, the lights went on:

Larry and Mike, two young teens, saw ads in the paper for the Palace Burlesk. They were big ads, bigger than what was showing at the big movies. Mikey cut out the ads and hid them in his math book. They often read them while waiting for the school bus in Larry's hallway.

Larry said: I dream of a girl with a milelong tit.
It wasn't a narrow, thin tit but his hands two feet and more apart motioning size and his messaging fingers measured a giant tit luscious and pushing all sanity out of his skull like one of those six hundred pound pumpkins, only two, massive with curly, hard nipples and one, mile, long. Cucurbita maxima.

They made a transgressive pilgrimage, in Buffalo, to Shelton Sodom of Busty Russell Square.
They wandered down Main Street far from the Sycamore 6 bus stop. There was a sign that said: the line forms here.
Larry said: I read that Busty Russell is here. She's got 50s! 50! Imagine that, rising and screaming, flooded with words. 50 inches! beauty, majestic, awesome, bedazzling, exalted, 50.

His ghost repeated over and over on each bead of the rosary: Goddamnit, my brain, I'm damaged, I fuckin broke it. a magic number: 50. what does it mean dictatorially drowning my skull thoughts? 50 Hail Marys.

Mikey imagined: He felt a form of longing and need, and a human formed, misty and transparent, and like he returned to Christmas in 1950, 50 living upstairs from Grandma B on May Street, 119 May Street. His parents were happy together. There was tinsel on the tree, lots of tinsel, tinsel flowed like Niagara Falls and the tinsel separated and a stockinged leg with a silver opened toed, high-heel appeared. He appeared in 50 someplace else, like a ghost, seeing brightly colored orbs, blue, yellow, yellow-white, ghost white streetlights lining the street and disappearing out beyond the truck junkyard, out beyond the train tracks.

The marquee blurted with flashing bulbous bulbs:

Busty Russell
Twice Daily   7 pm and 10 pm
Two complete shows
With Honey Bee and Tempest Storm
Featuring comedian Frank Merriweather

Frank told a joke something about Dial soap and how Dial was laid spelled backwards.
Every time I washed my hands.

d

♪ I rode a lion to town, use a rattlesnake whip
♪ Take it easy baby, don't give me no lip
♪ Who do you love?
♪ Who do you love?
♪ Who do you love?
♪ Who do you love?
♪ I asked my mother, what will I be?
Her mother asks him: what will you be, you know, for a job?
He says to she's mother: mattress tester.
He said to she: forever, if I live forever
I will love you forever
If I write poetry forever
If I make lines of poetry
One or maybe two will live forever
By mistake

e

Laff in the Dark Cryptomnesia

"Ghost hand, empty-handed form that uses esthetic and rye bread, rhythmic qualities such as photosynthetic, sound, cymbal of indefinite pitch, and meat, like pork, to evoke, or spell, meanings in addition to, the prostitute, prostatic, superficial, meaning and to summon the realm of ghosts where wiring automatically happens as if by automatic autoeroticism the magic of the hand moving as a Martian, or in a French, postcards, fashion, massage messages from romances of the subliminal imagination, derived largely empty from forgotten, or unknown fonts."
Her ghost said: you try too hard. give up the ghost.
His ghost said: my hand fell asleep.
Her ghost said: don't go apeshit.
His ghost said: it tingles.
The Tingler is a 1959 American horror film that tells the story of a scientist who discovers a parasite called a tingler. Ladies and gentlemen, please *do not* panic. But scream! Scream for your lives! The tingler is loose in *this*.
[Instructions: Scream louder than Fay Wray. Scream louder than Yoko Ono. Duel Duet.]

Her ghost said: Red-handed has its origin in the Buffalo epic poem about a Viking boat race on Lake Ontario. The first to touch the shore of Olcott Beach would become sovereign of healing, death, royalty, the gallows, knowledge, battle, sorcery, poetry, frenzy, and the alphabet. The letter, I, errant, guaranteed her win by cutting off his hand and throwing it to the shore ahead of her slithering suitors and laughing to spite my face.

One handed catch.
I can do it with one hand tied behind my back.
You only need one hand.
Good with one hand.
I've got a good hand.
Give her a hand.
I've got to hand it to you.
Take matters into your own hands.

> Try your hand at this.
> Out of hand.
> A ghost with one hand clapping [actualize this in some fashion].
> Sit on your hands [actualize this in some fashion].
> Stop playing with yourself [actualize this in some fashion].

Ghostly incant: all my long sorry days brim with bottomless sorrow, like the evening's sorry looking shadows long of disposed condoms on his clothesline, clothes pin.

Her ghost incant: I go with the flow, life is short and I can't wait for your forever, in your dreams, Sluggo, that just ain't gunna F'n happen in your lifetime, don't let the door hit you in the ass, oh well, life goes on, rock n' roll, the grass is greener on the other side of lemon aide, too much lemon triggers heartburn when the esophageal sphincter between your esophagus and stomach doesn't function, in the mid-19th century lemon was used as a colloquial term for a tart, or slang for a sucker, or a loser, a dim, stems from the idea that he is easy to suck the juice out of, by 1909 lemon was also firmly established in American slang as a term for something worthless, especially a broken or useless item fobbed off or, an unsuspecting wooer.

In your dreams: cow-eyed cow Psyche she remembers she bit him up, rides in brightly painted sheet metal passenger boats blue and Easter yellow Leda swan feathers and red and blue and yellow giant sea fish sheet metal boats pass through dark passages at Crystal Beach Amusement Park's psyche a ride for two called The Tunnel of Love or Laff in the Dark, one in the same, six of one or a half dozen of the other and hearing her scream bloody murder.
[Instructions: Scream louder than Fay Wray. Scream louder than Yoko Ono. Duel.]

In your dreams: he sweaty held her guiltless guillotine ride tickets, a real sweet treat a hand-full, and red-handed them over to Charon the Toad, the golden-eyed toad of doors, trapped, caught, the tip of his pecker in his zipper, blush, his box shaped boat swan, and swan feathers, she used to conceal her weapon.

Her ghost incant: silent as a clam, calm clam, calm clam, speaking eye to eye I couldn't believe my eyes, raised eyebrows, bows, two scoops, her eyes, pine, eyeing madly the eye candy, the once over, do me a flavor, I'll keep an eye out for you ocular prosthesis, an eye in the hand is worth an empty bush, some bush, giving him, the eye of the storm, seeing eye to eye, private, eye, and then I asked him with my eyes, to ask again. you can. if you can. you may. let. lemon.

Tunnel vision. Spook alley. The ghost said: no repeat rides. First, we floated like ghosts through a narrow corridor adorned with Exit signs, green lights, exposed wiring, flooded mouths, swallow deeply, wait, the daddy longlegs has the world's most powerful venom, but fortunately her fangs are so small they bite just blossoms into a June strawberry-stippled blemish, bruised, semi-dark, yellow and blue, and black, blacklash, lashes, his eyes shut, smut, he felt something on his arm, crawling, creepy-crawly, he tingled tingle, tingle all the way.
His ghost said: I felt the spider's schvantz moving up my arm.
[Instructions: Scream louder than Fay Wray. Scream louder than Yoko Ono. Duet.]

In your dreams: he startled and shivered and pissed into the wind as she started to pee by heating sugar and spinning the liquefied teaseathon sugar out through tiny holes where it solidified in thin strands of spun sugar glass that cut him deep and clean into his palms and spider webs her pin-up stitchery of black and white silk threads of time seam out of control her final night cotton candy curls contains mostly the air of lingerie, and the old silent air stuffy of the old mummy room in the basement of the Field Museum in Chicago, and your cold, stale hands heating in all his hot internal organs, removed, pull out, except in time, his hot oversized heart wrapped in plastic Band-Aid plastic sheer strips, stuffed with cotton balls, packed with White Cloud Cotton Balls Jumbo Size 100% pure 200 Count from Target, and a nude witch poured salt on his wound, sodium chloride, table salt he sprinkled table salt on the tail feathers of her sparrow, pass the salt and pecker shaker, sodium carbonate, sodium bicarbonate, and sodium sulfate her natron blush bowling on Tuesday, after work, tryst.

> *Smin, smin* opens thy mouth. One pellet of natron.
> Thou shalt taste its taste in front of the *sḥ-ntr*-chapels. One pellet of natron.
> That which Horus spits out is *smin*. One pellet of natron.
> That which Set spits out is *smin*. One pellet of natron.
> That which the two harmonious gods spit out is *smin*. One pellet of natron.
> Thou hast purified himself with natron, together with Horus and the Followers of Horus. Five pellets of natron from Nekheb.
> Thou purifiest herself. Horus purifies himself. One pellet of natron.
> Thou purifiest herself. Set purifies himself. One pellet of natron.
> Thou purifiest himself. Thoth purifies himself. One pellet of natron.
> Thou purifiest herself. The god purifies herself. One pellet of natron.
> Thou also purifiest herself. One pellet of natron.
> Thy mouth is the mouth of a sucking calf on the day of his birth.

Her ghost incant: I cried wolf so cry me a Niagara river, tonight Mikey Milky Way boy no sense crying over spilt milk, when hell freezes over I offered her my hand that bit me, you got my hopes up in the palm of my hand, up, just where I want him, *I'll See You in My Dreams* (film - 1951) forever eternity no song lyric available, she made me, an offering, don't hold your breath, asshole, I walked away, empty handed.

f

Ghosts of June Ghost Syndical

Weather Goddess Autumn Lewandowski, meteorologist for Channel 7, whispers: a thunderstorm made form by my May wand, also known as an electrical storm, a lightning storm, or a thundershower, is a type of storm characterized by the presence of finger lightning, and strong winds, and its acoustic effect on his brain's atmosphere known as auditory hallucination.
Igor stole his diseased brain.
I'm sorry. It was a mistake. I'm sorry. It's broken.
It was the wind. It was on my mind.
The stitched ready body rises raised up on a platform up into her summer rose, June, solstice, thunderstorm.
Her ghost said: these luxuriances only formed his skin, scarcely covered the words and spirals, of muscles and arteries beneath whom with such infinite pains and care I had endeavored to form.
A white foundation garment is an undergarment designed to temporarily alter the ghost's body shape.
While inspecting Niagara Square a sudden June storm whipped as cream like with spells by witches, of June rain ghost automatic speakings, in laundromats speakings spook spoke in veils, in ravels and knots and mesh ghosts to Ravel's "Bolero."
I now also began to collect the materials for my new creation, and this was to me like the torture of single drops of water continually falling on my head.
The National Science Foundation reports that up to 40 percent of the population will hear voices at some point in their lives.
These clear facts are clear. 1) Ghosts often select a favorite letter for their utters of pain, grief, and/or anger, e.g., j: J-J-J jjjjjj elongated variously in pain, grief and/or anger. 2) Ghosts sometimes pick a wail word, e.g., sink: sssssSssss...innnnn...etc. elongated variously in pain, grief and/or anger.
Her ghost said: he muttered some inarticulate sounds.
   Ghost utter of a letter like L leading into an utter of a word like restroom or lilac (Syringa vulgaris).

It Was an Early June Afternoon
Drama
Characters: stuck remnants.
Scene: A bench in Niagara Square in Buffalo, New York.
Memory a, leafless tree.

Prelude of Ghost Speakings:

What you wished was me to begin with the letter Q.
That's as hard as Z but Z is kinda easy, you know.
Almost impossible.
You can go for days without seeing any letter Qs.
Nothing either begins with the letter X.
It's a kiss, forever.
You can almost forget and then, there, back again.
Always comes back around to bite you.
I will need the sacrament laid upon my tongue.
The nun said: never, allow *It* to touch your teeth.
Never, *It's* the way I'm built.
What you're waiting for was.
It always gets away.
Kissing falling water falling your fingers open, a jar, like air.
A falling glass hitting the stone floor.
Like in the wind, leaves.
Let go.
Easy-peasy.
You might not feel the same, but do you forget?
Two can forget the same need.
Can't.
If you were there you're here.
Don't forget what lasts.
Don't forget want lasts.
What we did we do.
♪ There she was just a-walkin' down the street, singin' do wah diddy diddy dum diddy do.

His ghost said: she ate a Niagara County McIntosh apple, red, *It Amanita mascara.*
A ghost said: you only hear what you want to hear.
She was Our Lady of Ghosts. There in the grotto on Pine Ridge Road, by the nuns.
Sounds like! By cupping your hand to an ear, you'll signal to your team that you're only acting out a word that sounds like the one you're working on.
When lightning struck in the same place twice, it was the whammy, auditory and visual distortions stuck as they were fixed in time with mood changes, euphoria, relaxation, ataxia, and seeing and hearing lots a ghosts.
      Ghost utter of a letter like Q leading into an utter of a word, like Cheerios or Chaucer, as it appears in the mind.
A ghost said: there's no such ghost as a free lunch.
A ghost said: why buy the cow when the ghost is free.
      Ghost utter of a letter like E.
Her ghost said: you're invisible, right? this just doesn't make any sense? you're not here.
His ghost said: here you go. it's what you wanted, all the time, right? for all time.
Her ghost said: if I am seeing it, why isn't it here?
His ghost said: what you see you saw.
Her ghost said: hand saws have sharp teeth.
A ghost said: seasaws.
Her ghost said: don't saw me in half.
His ghost said: we are hear, hear it. every word a ghost.
      Ghost utter of a word like, perhaps, explore.

Her ghost said: feel around, it's your birthday gift.
His ghost said: under Buffalo is Circe's palace.
She led him into the Underworld where protected in a red circle of sheep's blood and fire engines and lipstick, the spirits of the dead surrounded him.
♪ Blue moon, you knew just what I was there for.
Elastic waistband.
He got so frightened he almost crapped his pants.

She undoes the snaps and hooks of a word like poetry and they are mechanical, the darkness slowly flimsy falls, looted onto, to the floor revealing the unraveling breeze, Aeaea.
A haruspex she inspected my entrails and channeled his spirits into forms.
She used VO5.
All twisted all he could think of was a Penelope saved is a Penelope earned.
Her ghost said: down the hatch, in one end and out the other, here's to you, forever as far as the ghost flies, in one forever ear and out the other, ever ear, what we do we will do forever what we did.

Speakings began (at random audience or readers perform the evoking noises*): The Fountain of the Innocent Frogs was erected on the occasion of King Henry II's solemn entry into Paris in 1549. Jean Gijon adorned it with lighthearted reliefs evoking her water nymphs with (*evoking noises begin:) simple crooks, isolated sounds, or complex and long, sometimes foaming laughs, sounds like bells, cackles, trills, cuckoo calls, barks, whistles, flute, meows, grunts, buzzing, zooms, hums, started engines, hammers hitting an anvil, rowing, and drum beats and breeding ghosts enchanted in her nymphaeum crayfish gonads located in my heart appear as a pair of tubular structures in my I a church that combines in my heart into her single mass to celebrate my selves as her moon Eucharist.
♪ Bom, ba-ba-Bom, ba-Dang-a-Dang Dang, a-Ding-a-Dong Ding.

Zoooooooooooooooooooooooooooooommmmmmmmmmmmmmmmmm moooooooooooooooooooooooooonnnnnnnnnnnnnnnnnnnnnnnnnnn-nnnnnnnnnnnnnnnnnnnn.
The Maid of the Mist was originally a Haudenosaunee myth where a young ex, hoping to pull the plug, gets into her canoe and enters the wanting waters above Niagara Falls.
From Luna Island he heard her, prolonged, low, inarticulate, through Hell's Half Acre, over the Bridal Veil, into his thirsting kisser of Aeolus. The Cave of the Winds, was a natural cave behind Bridal Veil Falls, was 130 feet high, was 100 feet wide, and was 30 feet deep. The 70 mph winds underneath the falls were a June storm. The cave was obliterated

in a massive 1954 rockfall.
His ghost said: O Three Stooges: Niagara Falls! slowly I turned, step by step, inch by inch....
O is a hug.
Local officials estimate 20 to 40 people commit suicide at Niagara Falls every year.
The Maid of the Mist amusement ride now collects the suicides from the turbulent waters beneath the falls, the American Falls, the Horseshoe or Canadian Falls, the Bridal Veil Falls.
It is believed that Niagara is a derivative of the Iroquoian word, Onguiaahra, meaning the narrow water passage that flows, north from Lake Erie to Lake Ontario.
Niagara Square in Buffalo, New York, was hence named by Joseph Elliot in 1804. Elliot's final years were marred by serious mental problems. He was admitted to an asylum in New York City where he died in 1826 by hanging himself. His ghost songs about as wind, and haunts Niagara Square.

    (at random audience or readers perform the haunts*)
In 1825 the three Thayer brothers were hung in Niagara Square in the presence of 30,000 Buffalo citizens after the brothers were convicted of murdering Mr. Love. Their three ghosts haunt Niagara Square sometimes (* haunts begin here:) grunting or buzzing, boozing, zooming hums, started engines, roofers up upon a roof, the sounds of bowling allies, and seagulls.
Strike!

Speakings: In Buffalo, Niagara Square is a circle and there erected President William McKinley's memorial. Completed in 1907, the McKinley Monument is an obelisk made of Vermont marble, 96 feet tall with fountains, and giant sleeping white lions, and turtles at its base. Carl Sandburg wrote a poem about the monument called: "Slants at Buffalo, New York."
In a Swedish accent Sandburg's ghosts recites: "Four lions snore in stone at the corner of the shaft."
His ghost said: the lions are like the obelisk's balls. Sandbag didn't write that.

Speakings: Morgan, Rockefeller, and Carnegie did not give a fuck about working people. Leon Czolgosz defended working people and did not give a fuck about Morgan, Rockefeller, and Carnegie. McKinley was groomed and elected by Morgan, Rockefeller, and Carnegie to do their political bidding. McKinley was assassinated in Buffalo while attending the Pan-American Exposition in 1901 by Polish-American Leon Czolgosz, an introverted young poet, an ex-steelworker, an anarchist who rented a room of passions and possessions on Broadway near Woltz.

Charging a quarter, Buffalo's successful entrepreneurs attempted to electrocute an Indian elephant at the Pan-Am. It failed. It was reported that Leon Czolgosz was in the bleachers. Admission is not refundable.

McKinley was shot in the Hall of Music. ♪ It's just a shot away.

Leon Czolgosz incanted: I possessed by imagination, I addicted to delusional poetry, I feel the shaped curve opening of the poem, I gift digressions and rants, I compose in Anarcho-syndicalism with equal and permitted forms juxtaposed, I lay my eggs in strings attached to vegetation and fountains, I hatch into tiny black flag tadpoles, tadpoles are alphabet letters in motion, alive, forming, I metamorphose, I of boiling imagination real in the political, poetical, rebellical, umbilical, sociological, poetatagical, I am real one with the realm of the poem.

When Leon pulled the trigger, he was 28.
McKinley was 58.
Morgan lived to 75.
Carnegie lived to 83.
Rockefeller lived to 97.
When Leon pulled the trigger, he shouted: Psai Krew!
      Ghost utter of the word psai.
Psai krew! is a nineteenth century Polish peasant oath and in translation means bad dog's blood.
In Belorussian psh means ghost.
      Ghost utter of the word krew.
Trigger was a palomino horse made famous in American Western films

with his owner and rider, cowboy star Roy Rogers. Trigger was born in 1932.
Close the barn door before the horse gets away.
Trigger finger.
Elicit.
Roy Rogers asked Dale Evans to pull his trigger.
Trigger was stuffed and mounted and was on exhibit for 40 years. At auction someone paid $266,000 for Trigger.
Dale Evans wrote "Happy Trails."
♪ Happy trails to you, until we meet again.

McKinley was shot in the Hall of Music.
In Belorussian psh means ghost.
      Ghost utter of the word krew.

On October 22, 1976, a chilly afternoon in downtown Buffalo, a man committed suicide by jumping from the top of Buffalo's City Hall. A strong gust of ghostly wind came along, changed his trajectory, and impaled him on the flagpole above the main entrance. Completed in 1931, the Art Deco City Hall stands 398 feet from bottom to top. On the 28th floor is an observation deck, a narrow walkway that serpentines around the building's exterior, allowing a majestic 360-degree panoramic view of Buffalo. Shortly before 3 PM Robert Jackson stood on the tower's east side, positioned directly above the building's main entrance and looking east toward the McKinley Monument.

      (A number of instruments play off stage)
      (At random perform the restless noises*)
Speakings: Restless ghosts in Niagara Square gently bellow like *church bells, choirs, cackles, trills, cuckoo calls, barks, whistles, flutes, trumpets, and moons.
      Ghost utter of the word moon. Bark.

His ghost aside: he felt guilty that he wasn't writing a ballade about McKinley's assassination or the monument. he thought he could do a better job than Carl Sandburg. he thought about poeming Robert Jackson and how Jackson was a dandelion seed pushed and pulled by her winds. if only he could have sown into the future. if only… he would be really famous by now. maybe even living in the Elmwood Village or Ellicottville! he was always still so young and so stupid and so still deeply fueled by the bull spirit of romance. and still so in grief. he weeps deeply, a falls for metaphors.

I am not me.
Don't blow a fuse.
Innumerable sounds rang in my ears.
Jesus Christ, what do you want from me?
Easy access.
I found too much.
We shall live in many forms.
♪ Yummy, yummy, yummy, I got love in my tummy.
♪ We all live in a yellow submarine.
It was 1932 and the movie was black and white. Imhotep the mummy searches for his lost love, searches for his incarnate lost love.
I am Ankh-es-en-amon.
There is a crossroads in time.
Should we meet?
Can't help it.
A strange multiplicity of sensations seized me.
I am thy creature.

His ghost said: wish to hear my new poem?
Her ghost said: come to the lawn fate and I'll play with your wiener.

Ghost utter of the word wiener.
Do wah diddy, I live in the city.

His ghost aside: long ago when ridiculous things had matter. the list was endless. he woke nauseated already in a day's guilt. he felt guilty about eating buttered toast with apple jelly. he remembered thinking how a shapely woman's legs in church reminded him of Coca Cola bottles. if only he could wed a witch.
His witch wish was an appropriated apparition captive.
Her ghost said: sit, on my three-legged stool. I have a three-legged pot.
If only an optical illusion if, if only he wasn't a prisoner of his wiener.

Niagara is an American 1953 film noir thriller starring Marilyn Monroe. It was one of Fox's biggest box office hits of that year.
The association between Marilyn and the Falls was made complete by one of the poster ads for the film, which depicts a larger-than-life Marilyn lying atop the Falls with the water flowing over her scantily clad body.
Unlike other film noirs of the time that were filmed in black and white, *Niagara* was filmed in three-strip Technicolor.
Marilyn's character is named Rose, and in the film, she wore a red wiggle dress.
When the character played by Casey Adams spies Rose's entrance in this dress, he remarks, "Get out the fire hose!"

Guilty, ghosts quickly do often spontaneously vanish. Hidden Corrective Concealer. Luxury Performance Makeup. A creamy, weightless and moisturizing concealer that blends easily into her skin for an undetectable finish.

His soliloquy: You are thin clouded glass. I am a glass soul slipper lights on and off, flickers, fails, falls slips from, filled slipped flipped through my brimming fingers and slept, cuts her slip into 24 frames per second, or a glass of milk glass licked chipped glass, cut her lip, milked form a breath breathe spilled spilt spell her white slip slept all day, my tiny teeth spit the snow, fell, out, fall out, fall quietly my tiny tongue fingers slip around my neck, broke, broken glass on the stone floor, be careful, you'll cut yourself, he fell and broke his neck, we necked for hours in the Paramount Theatre on Main Street, and when I fell I broke my ass, he felt bankrupt, he got a feel, caress her naked foot fell, his foot upon her neck, slip knot necking, noose, her polymerized nylon-based blend of synthetic fibers made from adipic acid and hexamethylene diamine chemically combined to form a nylon salt thermoplastic fiber, the thief wore a stocking mask.

Her soliloquy: Half-assed his open moon esophagus jellyfish tongue, my mouth muse milking cows, come home, wholly white moon in holy plumage mooing cow swan schvantz uprising blood moon, blue moon, super moon, the June strawberry moon so named because of the short

moon season for gathering strawberries, I command his plummet over an endless edge, his swan plumage, his mute swan arrowed, sacramental swan muse worn this thin thin scapular, his plumber comes with promises Promethean promiscuousness, against God with no promise of salvation, he left tangled on the bathroom sink my salvaged ghost moon, white washcloth, will not fly beautiful like a beautiful salivating lake witches of migrating swans, and moons, into Niagara Square, when the chimes come for him, come time chime, crime, it's a crime, half pass a monkey's ass and a quarter to his balls.
                (A few instruments play off stage)

The ghost of Czolgosz incants: the McKinley monument is an abomination.
                Ghost utter of the word abomination.
The ghost of Czolgosz incants: I died, meaningless has meaning, a rendering process simultaneously dries the material and separates the fat from the bone and protein, and there is a new form, there are no dead ends only, only my liberation.

Uprising through the cracks about the fountain's base uprising dandelions.
Native to North America.
Split.
A nuisance weed of the daisy family, with a rosette of leaves, bright yellow flowers followed by a globular head of seed with downy tufts, and stems containing a milky latex.
Spread, squeezed into minute cracks.
Eyesores.
In the seams and cracks of monuments can be annoying and unsightly and can be considerably more difficult to remove than weeds in a flower bed.
"Ozymandias."
A flourishing dandelion population will break apart the cement and eventually the monument will become a ghost.
The dandelion, from the French dent-de-lion: lion's teeth.

Leon F. Czolgosz suffered the punishment of death inflicted by the application of electricity. Only his conscious life was absolutely destroyed the instant the first contact with the electricity was made. The strength of the current is not stated.
Leon Czolgosz's body was placed in a plain, black casket and doused with sulfuric acid and his remains disintegrated within 12 hours leaving only bezoars.

A bezoar is a lost stone. No one remembers, where the bezoar was originated, some imagine Persia. Alexander had a bezoar ring. A bezoar is a movie starlet. A bezoar is a bombshell, is Beltane. She had a dandelion yellow bezoar ring. No one really recalls, really, what color the stone might be. Some explorers note that bezoars were the fingernails of the Yeti or originate in the skulls of the North American common toad.
The bezoar gives the eyes of the *Bufo americanus* their gold color.
Her ghost said: Bufo? you mean toads are named for Buff-low?
Ian Fleming wrote that toad sweat is an aphrodisiac.
The Toad God is a supernatural creature worshipped as a god by a mysterious and bizarre Mayan tribe that existed long ago before the sinking of Atlantis.

I left.
Did you leave?
I never got your letter.
Which one, A, B, C...?
The monster might depart forever.
What's left?
Left without leaving a trace.
Olfactory apparition.
The elephant house.
Ammonia.
Deep Heat muscle rub and very mild cheddar.
Lilacs.
Leave your key.
The process by which floral organs turn into foliage.
Leave it to Beaver.

Mr. Toad indulges his impulsive desires.

A large toad with pulsating, multicolored eyes, which emits a loud, ominous buzzing noise has the power to hypnotize almost any living thing at will.

Toads react to certain areas of the home or seem to react to something they cannot see.

They hide from ghosts.

When her parents were out of town, I looked, felt around and found no toads, in the bathroom, dining room, in her bedroom, and none in the kitchen, under the sink, within her humming, her hammering, zooming among her spoons, a rugby match, a train's whistle at 2 AM, whooping swans.

Romantic, she was haunted by hallucinations.

                I see you in the dark.

            The magician sawed her in half.

He heard:

♪ So how could I dance with another?

♪ Whooooh.

An Amphibian Emerges in Cheektowaga

It might have been something in the water in Cheektowaga, near Pine Ridge Road.
Or something buried in barrels in the Walden fields out by the railroad tracks.
In his skull he felt unbound spring cattails, swamp, night, leach black, peeping Promethean repetitions, reptiles, pollywog ponds, and the words on his red pack Pall Mall cigarettes in waiting rooms.
It was a form of paradise these little writhing writing black spots in the middle of transparent jelly blobs.
All filmed in Technicolor yellow and blue, like a bruise floating on the field's pit-like puddle pools.
It, has to do with the thin-film indices of refraction, between life's oil, a form of makeup, make believe, and his ghostly water below.
Because of the way the light bends and reflects at the point where the two red meat met in his trance bushes, an interference pattern like a loaded rainbow, crime, such a shame.
Train oil spewed on a small pond like shadows, hotfoot circles expanding vowels and liver jaundice yellow, eye yellow, and blue, alcohol contusions, last call toad breeding, hematoma, his skin damaged by trauma, allowing his blood to sleep, hemorrhage into a Kleenex tissue, white cotton handkerchief.
Blood black as his interior cranium's sin skin tight hold, me like Spandex: a synthetic fiber or fabric made from a magic polymer containing polyurethane, tight, to him, hooks in, in lungs, stupid heart, all about his skin prick, endless loss of sleep, in sleep with letters slowly losing their tails.
While sleeping, he weeps sleep, sleep, he sleeps:

He Sings

♪ Pollywogs
♪ Pollywogs
♪ Pollydogs
♪ Polygamy
♪ Polygayou

♪ Polywoogs
♪ In my wet shoes
♪ From my wet brain
♪ Flows out my drain
♪ That is my mouth
♪ Out my bone
♪ That is my dick
♪ Out my ass
♪ I'm sure to flunk
♪ My writing class

Her Song:

In my dark and lucid France
Skilled his slippery shapely ants

g

A Cheese and Banana Apparition

Butter yellow cheese fungus as ol' as time herself.
His ghost said: yellowy butter, flour, water warm water, and these two hands to kneed, need thee, dough.
    (chorus)
♪ Some fungus his is used
♪ To make strange tastes
♪ To make strange tastes
♪ Some fungus his is used
Warm like tub water June, on the finger lake necklace shore, in late warm June like warm bath water, kneed and knot, his finger finger waves.
    (chorus)
♪ Some fungus his is used
♪ To make strange sounds
♪ To make strange sounds
♪ Some fungus his is used
♪ To string the words together

Plot:
Her ghost said: in collage I am gunna take up hands-on ocean cartography.
His ghost said: I will be infected, ill-gifted, given in, slender veldt gazelle, give, away, Scheherazade gave away large curds of cottage cheese!
Her ghost said: you think you know everything; you think you read all the books or something?
In a spell her ghost told her sister: he, has the black tongue of a troll, he, laps waving my terrified toaster, my shore eyes, my black shoes, and tub butter, he, is using me, he, uses his knead me into a hypnotized

stupor, and I, pretend to be bewitched, I, am in my mouth, June, am spell bound, I, have no sin, shame, and he, may feel me, at the movies.

Her ghost said: not all mold is dangerous and ♪ My love became a funeral fire.
His ghost said: I never had her faded swimsuit by Lanz, with yellow floral on white cotton, and the fitted silhouette, cut with a bodice that has princess seamlines, each has been boned to help the bodice stay in place, the back has a tie for closure on the back of the top.

Critical response:
Her ghost said: can you explain what you're thinking?
    (chorus)
♪ We all live in a yellow submarine
♪ Yellow submarine, yellow submarine.
When John Lennon had his first trip on LSD, he described George's house as being a submarine.
Donavan wrote the line: ♪ Sky of blue and sea of green.
Donavan wrote: ♪ Electrical banana goin to be the very next craze.
Because of Donovan's "Mellow Yellow," a rumor began that banana peels contained LSD!
Smokin dried banana peels behind the garage, his ghost did not see any racing giraffe.
Keep your eyes peeled.
She began to peel off her outer skin.
See the ghost whites of his eyes.
I seen something in the dark.
They were just we.
Touched.
He's touched.
Impure thoughts, and desires lemon cheesecake.
Say cheese.
Cheesecake photography.
Touching a ghost gives your hand a nasty sizzle, so, quick as a flash, you drop it.
Cheese dip.
Say please, first.

♪ Come mister tally man tally me banana.
Cheese may prevent cavities.
Orange you glad I didn't say banana.
There is, of course, the naturally yellowed cheddar from milk of June, grass-fed summer cows, and those moomers tend to produce a naturally yellower cheese.
There are 74 conditions associated with hallucinations.
♪ Electrical banana is bound to be the very next phase.
Roaming hands and Russian fingers, the, merry-go-round, round and round the mulberry bush, the monkey cheesed the weasel.
Ghosts murmur: on the end of his hands were the 11 Finger Lakes, from east to west: Otisco, Skaneateles, Oswaco, Seneca, Keuka, Canandiague, Honeoye, Canadice, Hemlock, and Conesus.

The act:
It was by Keuka Lake, in June, to be his mellow June larvae nymph, his Holstein June dairy goddess, I, my cow-maid moons, I, made me butter all over wadding wedding summer, bullet, it is all there is in black and white yellow, his release yellow sundress, spoiled rotten her sunfish jaguar yellow, wading in yellow egg yolks, and hooked, warm water in the shear water, yellow shimmer wiggle, and black, blue hook barbed, and yellow, high-carbon steel hooks, one brittle, one forgiving yellow, I will not forgive, never, you, need, yellow or leave, fish remember who brought you, the last dance, gone but not forgotten doctors, demographers, psychiatrists, researchers, social reformers, policy makers, futurologists, scientists, and pseudoscientists said: an elephant never forgets.
Her ghost said: smells like spoiled milkin here, or something like ghosts.
      The pale-yellow swimsuit dried on the hood of my
          yellow Ford Impala
            fox tail
         antennae of the race

Apparition h: The Pasterka Syndical

Pasterka is a midnight church Mass celebrated between the 24th and 25th of December at St. John Gualbert's Roman Catholic Church, down from the Dairy Queen on Walden Avenue, down from by Okonowski's funeral parlor.
Larry's ghost reported: Okie takes naked pictures of the women bodies! Hollywood Jones also lived in the neighborhood, and Mark's ghost said: he's got naked pictures of guys and guys dressed up as chicks, with lipstick and black eyeshit on their eyes.
Pasterka or Shepherds' Mass or Midnight Mass is a reference to the shepherds on Christmas Eve who late in the evening encountered millions of angels or ghosts ablaze in the open sky like shark teeth. The angels like ghosts was flying around like snowflakes, headed to church, and horning gold trumpets about goats and sheep and baby Jesus: ♪ hoooooooooooo.
    (Anyone with a trumpet may trumpet: now.)
Larry's ghost said: snow is angel snap.
Danny's ghost said: Lilly Bo Peep was boned by a sheep, or was that Old Mother Hubbard? I ain't so good at the poetry.
She haunted his every memory a haunting, haunting him, his universe with a soap on a roped snapping turtle snapper and round red rabid rain bricks, foreplay colanders, and flaming paper clips of excited opossum nun ticks biting hooks into his scrotum.
Her ghost said: SHURrrrrrrrrrrrrrrrrrrrrrrreeeeeeeeeeeeeeeeeeK.
Larry's ghost said: shepherds pork the sheep.
Danny's ghost said the sheep went: BaaaaaaaaaaaaaaaaaaeeeeeeeeeeeeeeeK.
Naked Angels was a biker movie made in 1969.

The Incident of a Circle of Teens

Christmas Eve evening in front of St. John Gualbert's: Enter all ghosts and their people and more unrelated ghosts, a whole shithouse of ghosts, and various smoking mid teen teen boys and teen girls all beautiful as young white-tailed deer emerging form from the forest forming a circle, skinny and entering the dark forest, smelling of meadow damp, smiling and wet as Saturday afternoon cheerleader car wash sponges. Shepherds

in their Sunday clothes stargaze blind into the starry starry sky light
liquid and moon light waiting a mood and moan. The teens smoke their
cigarettes and flick, their butt ends into the endless audience.
A teen ghost said: this should be an Olympic event.
A teen ghost said: we should have our own Olympics.
A teen ghost said: the Walden Olympics.
A teen ghost said: the cigarette toss is my best sport.
A teen ghost said: there should be an old woman scream competition.
when an old woman walks by scream as loud and as strangely as you
can. three points if she says something. two points if she turns. one point
if she shakes her head. zero if she just keeps shuffling.
The teens continue to smoke their cigarettes and flick their butt ends
into the audience. They squirm.
    (Scream for a duration of time screaming all forms of ghost screams.)

Eve was beautiful, and neither was I innocent of one word, one sound,
one next to her an other me, as a magician could cast and the would
spell, begins and opens and binds. Her bandage wrapped body is
raised through the roof of the church. Lightning strikes a kite sending
electricity through her body. Henry and Pretorius remove her white
bandages and help her to stand outside the church before Mass begins.

On Mogen David concord so buzzzed so we were so bombed toasted,
cooked, and hammered it was Christmas Eve swelled with birds or
angels, spelled her lips flew nothing said on each rosary bed, bead, of red
roses tormented by eyes my wishing where my eyes were shooting ache
and awe and I put the gun to my head next to an other. I almost died of
thirst. I gave her my eye, the eye. Mimir. Ears breathe in ancient Egypt.
The Ba was her soul, an imagined white dove of sound.

Danny bought wine for us at Walden Liquors cause he had fake I.D.,
and Larry got so drunk on Zombie wine he felled in the tangle of hedge
bushes by the priest's house and got tangledmup so much he couldn't
get out and up was flapping about maybe like a frying flying fish outa
water or like Crazy Kenny the Piss when he had a seizure at the Thruway
Plaza. Larry waved at us from the backseat of the squad car. He was
smiling and laughing as if he just got published in the *Norton Anthology*

of Modern Poetry. Msgr. Frank saw but didn't give a shit cause he got drunk at the Cove Grille Saturday night, everyone knew, ask Mitsi, every Sarday, over on Alexander Street by the corner, and he was hungover.

A ghost said: I touched her ♪ Partridge in a pear tree.
He lied on X-Mas to his friend Larry in his swelled skull a sweetened hand makes a move, movie off he went for angels, white butterflies, wanted, wings, alive or dead his Billy the Kid unclean soul standing in the unmoving line for endless Confession.

The Encounter

From the misty midst of the crowd of worshippers outside a church on Christmas Eve her apparition appeared as an ever-appearing ghost appears forever.
She, a white butter lamb* on top of the hot stove** of humanity. ***
Or was I?

*The Malczewski Butter Lamb is a traditional Polish Easter symbol that was started in Buffalo, decades ago by Ma Malczewski in the Broadway Market.
** A synonym for stove is furnace. Most stoves are white enamel like ghosts.
*** The writing professor said: you are mixing things up here, hot and the winter white of Christmas, Easter and Christmas, humanity is too abstract a word, and it will not work, not do, incorrect, because it isn't a real, poem, and no one believes in ghosts.

His ghost mind speaking in the darked tongue nightnesses were screeching: eggs egg whites kneaded into with her vanilla.
He knelled in church on the red leather kneeler of knelling.
Dark wood and marble the seams on the marble of her legs.
Butter and blend.
Angel food cake gently spoon batter into an ungreased angel food cake pan with a removable bottom.
Smooth top.
Cut a knife through batter to release air bubbles in the syringe in the

blood stream Hypodermic bubbles will burst my heart his.
In his head occurs the fragrance of guilt killed all the red canaries.
They laid in mounds on the ground like dried cranberries.
Ocean Spray.

The Encounter Continued

Scene two: the sky was fueled with stars, and sleepy sheep, on a meadow, ghostly sheets, ice burgers.
If her gift, of giving, or, me, my, to eye seen, out of the corner, by the corner, of Doat and Gualbert Streets.

Saw, her, mirror, I, see, me, seen, her, were, and, I, was, a, wish, I, may, it, is, a, was, it, happening, too.

Harmony and haphazardly, small, is, flakes, of, it, if, it, or, were, it, to, I, fell, into, my, hands, a penny in a well, melt.

What, she, said, I, made, her, only, heard, up, by, mistake, mistaken, head, said, it, over, and, over, never, listened, to, intently, intensely, long, not, myself, or, her, things, that, were, spoken, eyes, look, down, looked, away.

He heard from the balcony of the church:
Even a man who is pure in heart.
And says her prayers on Christmas night.
May become a wolf when the wolfsbane blooms.
And the winter star is bright.

Danny's ghost said: the poem above, repeated, repeated, several times during the encounter.*
(*Reader repeat this moon, poem at your leisure anywhere in the remainder of the poem, and at home, also, as mood insists.)
In church the poem is chanted by werewolves.
He hears this poem, not once, but several times, and the legend of poet lycanthropy begins to creep and soak, and fall waiting into his being grief but did not close his eyes at the first star sight only saw it I see it I think

aluminum ostrich marinated mandrake magic.
He weeps stupidity.
They were all right.
He was wacked.

Words, I, hear, heard, of, off, the, top, of, one, after, an, again, another, as, I, only, was, I, want, to, want, hear, her, speak, nothing, never, more, than, a, hi, and, bye, see, you, later, alligator, fuck, off, or, sung, by the Byrds: ♪ We'll meet again, don't know where, don't know when.

His ghost said: it was over so sweet that fast, like a fart, and I was left with a scar mark of an electric iron, Proctor Silex non-stick, on my face, red, she could not illiterate read it as plain as her night on my face.

Her ghost said: want, you, saw, what, you, wanted, to, see, me, speak, you, can't, wait, hear, what, yourself, tick.
Himself a bomb.

Inside the church at Mass looking around at the angels on the ceiling and around the altar, gold and sky blue, altar white all the celestial gigantic ceremonial congressional ten commandenial, majesty, sheep and shepherds at the annoucemental, Larry's ghost said: I'm gunna put all beds in here.

The Other Encounter

A Teen Witch Unnoticed Ghost an Other on the Other Side of the Teen Circle or Her Want that was Unseen Teenage Seeing You Can Never Fight a Ghost Ever!

I've got some shit in my eye.
Are you blind?
Can't see in here, it's dark.
I thought I saw something.
Can't you see what's going on.
Face it.

> Left behind.
> Close the blinds.
> You had your head in the clouds, or your head up your ass, or your head in the sand.

His ghost said: if I were here. I am there.
Her ghost sang: ♪ See me, feel me, touch me, heal me.
His ghost still believes he may be destined to unlock the secret of immortality.
Her ghost often visits him: OOoowowooooowowowwwwooooooo!
His ghost excuses: but I am film, filament, figments and fragments.
You did not see me, her ghost, in a French maid outfit, at the stove speaking: you have to let the eggs cook, in the heat, in the hot butter.
Heated his addicted five fingers each with a different finger lack,
warm, heart, cold lips, slow, stupid, unimaginative, bovine, dense, dim dimwitted, and thick.
♪ He ain't got no distractions
♪ Can't hear those buzzers and bells
♪ Don't see lights a flashin'
♪ Plays by sense of smell.

Eutrophication, forever my fingers will haunt you forever, in Ethiopia in the Arc of the Covenant, in the sweetness of summoned ghosts, and in unicorns as my fingers in the dwell, in a confessional, confession, confidential confusion concussion.
The way you didn't see me, blind as an asshole in a coal mine.
Her ghost purrred to him: your lack of oxygen with my excessive Europa kisses I am vowed to you soaking up all of your oxygen and vowels and my vomit asphyxia while intoxicated you ruined my creation with his brain she grew in a lab somewhere at St. Joe's Hospital, AKA in the neighborhood: Sloppy Joe's.
To help him create a new creature, a woman, I cannot forgive me, and I will kill his fish and snails.
> (Scream for a duration of time screaming like all forms of the bride of Frankenstein screams.)
> He will reside in my presence of Penance.

> His lips crawl fool leaving a trail of my slime.
> Merry Christmas, fucker.

Her ghost said: I put sugar in his gas tank.

I

Crystal Beach Syndical

Location: Crystal Beach Amusement Park, Ontario, Canada.
Boasted one of the fiercest roller coasters: The Comet.
The Comet was a mile long twisting terror.
Teenage girls were often terrified of the Comet.
Filled with testosterone fueled balls and delusional sperm, the boys would ride the Comet without seat belts, unlocked safety bar, and with arms starched out above their heads, palms open, fingers spread.
Six or seven were ejaculated each season.
Girls reported that there was a sense of being watched or spied on at Crystal Beach.
Folk saw transparent blue apparitions walking along the beach front.
Ghosts were seen flittering like hummingbirds in the Comet's coaster trestles.
Hummingbird nests hang like the testicles of old men.
Ghosts particularly enjoyed the funhouse, which was called the Magic Palace.
In the Magic Palace, ghosts would pop-up out of the dark.
In the restrooms, you could catch the crabs at Crystal Beach.
There were glory holes in the bathroom stalls at Crystal Beach.
Ghosts scared the socks off comely Pat the Rag.
The Magic Palace had skirt blowers.
I was so embarrassed giving them a free show!
Leering around and panting at the Magic Palace, the boys would later ride the bumper cars, with their arms stretched way out at the inquisition, way out above their hormone stuffed heads.
Ogle Paul popped a rod.
One of the guys shot his wad.
Laff in the Dark was a tunnel ride.
Being a poet, his ghost said: and then my heart becomed a throbbing, stuffed moon, or sky Kleenex.
She stuffed Kleenex in her bra to make her boobs look bigger.

Crystal Beach Amusement Park occupied waterfront land in Crystal Beach, Ontario, beginning in 1888.
The Iroquois said the beach front was the haunt of Big Heads, demons without bodies that would fly about in summer thunderstorms and eat teenage boys.
The Big Heads said: djcbjshshdnzhhwjJshjslbwidjzje. Ooo^{ooooooo}.
Larry's ghost said: ghosts went: BoooooOOOoooOOOOOOObs.
Crystal Beach was a nude beach between 1920 and 1924.
Folk saw all sorts of floating figures on the beach, strange sounding birds, dogs barking at thin air, and a young girl wandering around in a blue, mist, raw, Thai silk, curtain, panel.
Her ghost said: BluuuuuuuuUU…uuuuuu.
Ghosts can turn off appliances at will and sometimes for no reason and nothin was wrong, the amusement rides at Crystal Beach would stop.
Folk said it was human error.
Folk said if you went into the water at night something would pull on you.
Larry's ghost said he would go into the water at night, and he hoped something would pull on his dick.
I didn't say so, but I thought about it for a few weeks.
Part of the amusement park buildings were sited on a natural sand dune, fifty feet high, and 1,200 feet long, parallel to the shore.
At night teenage couples would neck on the dune.
It was long rumored that a huge metallic object was buried beneath the dune and mysterious rays would zoom up through the sand and make some teens go all the way.
Folk said the rays were a kinda lemon color unknown fear radiation.
Her ghost inquired: can you explain what you think you are doing?
He was putty in her hands.
She had him wrapped around her finger like pink cotton candy around a paper cone.
Jim Morrison sang: ♪ Now touch me, baby-
♪ Can't you see that I am not afraid?
♪ What was that promise that you made?
In June the entire dune glowed a sweet and sweaty gooey lemon-lime green ray stuff.

On June 22, 1954, the *Buffalo Courier Express* headline read: "Crystal Beach Lights Torch Evening Sky." The story related that no natural cause for the lights could be identified and that scientists were looking into the phenomena.
Larry's ghost said that his brother's ghost said: they call the beach Condom Beach because there are rubbers all over.

Crystal Beach day in Cheektowaga: His ghost asked her to go out, again and again. A date is an edible fruit. When they were apart she would dissolve like Ivory soap, but she couldn't float like a regular ghost.
♪ Just like a ghost, you've been a-hauntin' my dreams.
Everyone piled into chicken fat yellow school buses and roared up over the Peace Bridge to Crystal Beach. It was about 13 miles, which was spooky. The number 13 symbolizes the death to the matter of oneself and the birth of the ghost. For the superstitious,13 brings bad luck or misfortune.
On the way to Crystal Beach you passed Old Fort Erie. During the war of 1812 over 1,000 men died in a battle at Old Fort Erie. The place was haunted. In 1912 someone counted 1,000 Trumpeter Swans (*Cygnus buccinator*) at Fort Erie Beach. Folk said they were ghosts.
Later the next week in American History class Sue P. told him he didn't look very happy wandering around Crystal Beach. He told Sue P. that he hated lines. Sue said she liked to drop snowballs onto pedestrians from the parking ramp on top of the Broadway Market. She ended up living in a forest someplace in Hawaii. She smoked pot. He liked going into the covered tunnel rides so no one would see him. He felt better in the dark, without violation, prying eyes. I don't see what I see want.

They waited for eternity at the Tunnel of Love. The swan boats hooked onto a bicycle chain kinda chain that pulled the swan car thought the water and made a sorta strange noise like clanking chains. The water was dark, fervent, and greasy. Mosquito larvae lived in the hot water and would wiggle insanely. The taste of mold was in the air. Mold tastes like cheese. A mold is a fungus that grows in the form of multicellular filaments called hyphae. In Crystal Beach the folk spelled mold: m o u l d. In line, his ghost wondered if he would get some tongue. Online, her ghost wondered if she would get some tongue. What was supposed to happen in the artificial night, who invented pliers, does a chicken have lips? Ergot is a form of mould. At Crystal Beach the Tunnel of Love ride was called Laff in the Dark. He put his hand through her cobwebs. Each 90-degree turn jerked the swan. Their nostrils deeply inhaled the frozen odor of dreams and June sticky ghost breath. The neurotropic action of ergot may cause hallucinations and irrational behavior, seizures, high fever, unconsciousness and the risk of leaky heart. In the dank and hot damp, mouldy make out pit, his ghost hot brain was filled with song:

♪ The dark and dank
♪ So, walk the plank
♪ The creepy secret dark and dim
♪ The thin the skin the rolling pin
♪ Rolled over him
♪ He could not win all frozen thick
♪ With fright and fear that made him sick
♪ And seconds quick away did tick and tick
♪ And in his pants, there was his dick
♪ He thought he ought but not get caught
♪ In Mortal sin cast into hell
♪ To squirm and burn so fast he fled
♪ Inside his head he found the poem
♪ That almost rhymed with protozoan

Find an excuse to touch her fingers, either by brushing her palm with yours or by giving her something to hold.
New lightbulbs that seem to blow out too quickly.
Switch the lights, switching on and off, fast, a 1960s nightclub with the Strawberry Alarm Clock playing "Incense and Peppermints."
Easy Off is an oven cleaner.
Her ghost said: if it is there, you see it, white as winter.
His ghost said: I always hear you, dusk in my skull, coupling boxcar, clash, birds, echoing, what music they make, Easter.
Her ghost said: your ears are so tiny. how can you hear anything? you never hear anything I say. listen for once in your life. you should clean the shit out of your ears. I talk and talk until I'm blue in my face.
Whispers are not caused by a rational explanation.

Bullet headlights were the secret chemistry in the air increasing in volume without any rational explanation.
Her also hearing a favorite song from a loved one who had crossed over.
♪ Ooh, eeh, ooh, ah, ah, ting, tang, walla, walla, bing, bang.
Hearing her voice itself then her form, his ghost said: her thoughts were a flower, transfiguration fruit of the moon loom, shadow tuba confessing, cardinals exhaustion, see she saw was, thin ghost of unfilled fall, boing! memory them, merry-go-round sheets with the eyes cut out, and horses unlit bones, plain yoga, Gypsy Rose Lee xylophone telephone, blossoms smash bleak cupcakes, later, her dress has a higher neckline and she is wearing a pearl necklace, still later, the necklace is gone, John Lemon sang "Norwegian Wood," in *This Island Earth* other scientists in the facility had been transformed and were exhibitioning a weird behavior,
♪ Listen, while I play, my green tangerine.
Her ghost said: this is just phlegm.
Her ghost said: is this, so, supposed to be about me? I don't get it?
His creative writing teacher said: this is so intensely personal that I, just, don't, know.
His ghost said: comet rhymed with commit.
He got a B.
He used Comet on his frying pan. It sorta shinned and he could almost see himself in it, kinda, like a distortion mirror, he was Loki.
It was just an experiment. It was meant to be a mistake. Mistakes can sometimes be good. I made a mistake. I am made of mistakes. I made a lifetime of mistakes. When he looked at his poems, he saw frolicking misprints. Mistakes will be made. He realized that his ambitions to win her endless love via poetry only resulted in his writing shit and craves. He vowed never to write again. He lied to her. He waited for Odin to send a wish maiden. He waited and waited but the bus didn't come. It was a lifetime of waiting, of wrong turns, of missteps, false starts, error, fault, grief, inaccuracy, guilt by omission, and his mind and notebooks fulla squiggly veils and vials of poetry. When he was scrambling to get out of the swan boat he slipped and was falling.
Her ghost said: only a miracle will save you.

Duck Pond was a game of chance.
His ghost picked up a yellow rubber duck from a flowing stream of a million smiling, laughing yellow rubber ducks.
On the bottom of the duck was a number.
If he was lucky and got the right number, he might win a huge stuffed huge blue horse.
Larry's ghost said: fuck it, the guys walking around with a gigantic blue horse and a blonde date, didn't win the horse. they were paid to do that, to lurid you to wanna play Ball Bingo.
Her ghost said: the gigantic stuffed horses were stuffed with cheap stiff straw, like from a barn, you know, like where Jesus slept.
Her ghost said: they were uncomfortable.
His ghost asked: like the scarecrow form from Oz whose head was stuffed with cheap straw and wanted, a brain?
His ghost said: most people don't want a brain.
Her ghost said: I'm kinda ascared.
The Oz film Manufacturing Company was organized to make movies of L. Frank Baum books. The company's second project was a film of *His Majesty, the Scarecrow of Oz*, produced at a cost of $23,500, and with a cast of 130, it was released in 1914. Things did not quite work out well.
Oh well, that's the nature of poetry.
Maybe you can get a Dover edition?
He picked up a yellow duck and on the bottom was the number six.
He won a Chinese handcuff.
Chinese handcuffs or a Chinese finger trap is a simple puzzle that traps the victim's fingers in both ends of a small cylinder woven from colorful bamboo. The single ended version sold as a girlfriend trap and has been available since at least 1870 when it was first advertised as a girl catcher.

Volsi was a Viking fertility god whom the pagans deified as a horse phallus.
Her ghost said: my girlfriend had a giant blue horse and she had it on her bed and she fell asleep with her head on the horse and it was hot and she sweated and when she woke up the side of her face was deep blue like the horse because the horse wasn't dyed good and with shit dye, not like Rit.
The sky became blue.

Once in a blue moon.
Blue water runs deep.
Rinso Blue.
Blue Oster Cult.
Out of the blue.
He knew it was all a blooper.
According to Crystal Beach legend, during the Prohibition era, a young girl who frequented the park had an affair with the boy who built the Comet, and kept it from her unsuspecting true-blue boyfriend, who later stabbed her to death while walking along the beach necklace below the roller coaster with her lover. In another version of the legend, the woman fell off the Comet, which she was riding with her lover. For some reason she was standing up.
Folk said she lifted her top up.
He, was stood up.
She, was held up.
He didn't know which end was up.
Reportedly, the park patrons and staff who saw the blue lady said they felt like they were breathing a kinda of sand that tasted like latex bubble gum and mould, m-o-u-l-d, specially on hot days.
Some folk saw her and quit.
Some folk didn't care cause they needed the money.
There was a 16 foot statue of Paul Bunyan at Crystal Beach.
He stood near the Comet.
He had blue pants.
People would pose between his legs.
He carried a sign that said: Having fun at Crystal Beach.
Larry's ghost said: Paul Bunyan's dick was a vestigial organ.
When she saw a guy walking around with a large stuffed blue horse, her ghost said: ooh la la.

In 1966 an accident caused a man on the Rocket to lose his eye. Apparently, he leaned his head too far out of the car and hit a support post. Police reported that the man had been drinking Mogen David Concord grape wine.
His lips were a deep blue grape color, like the wine dark Lake Erie.
Mogen David began making wine in Chicago in 1933.

MD 20/20 is called Mad Dog, a Concord Grape fortified wine.
He seemed to remember that Cheerios were also fortified.
Mad Dog came in a kiwi lemon-lime flavor.
If you drank Mad Dog, you would glow in the dark and see things that weren't there, and then later you didn't remember nothing.
After drinking Mad Dog, the poet said: It was obvious to me that I was her saucer flying out over Lake Erie and rapidly accelerated until I was enclosed in her fireball, in her invisible ray, and crashed into her water, and, I, exploded.

His ghost said, Crystal Beach often comes to mind.
Her ghost said, if there is no light in the darkness, how can you see my ghost?
His ghost said: purity is imperfect.
Her ghost said: 99 and 44%.
Her ghost said: do you think about me? do you miss me? I know you miss me.
His ghost said: I am missing.

At Crystal Beach the trash cans were thick wiry things all over the place with lots of flies buzzing around the garbage.
At Crystal Beach a pesky fly flew around her head.
His ghost said: I do these things, so I appear normal.
Loki turned himself into a fly and stole her necklace while she closed her eyes.
He liked going into the covered tunnel rides, so no one could see him.
In the cars on the Haunted Mansion ride to improve the effect and give a sense of journey, dark rides frequently change direction. Sudden curves give a sense of surprise and allow new scenes to surprise. The rides may also feature sudden ascents or descents to further the surprise, auditioning, of the finger puppets.

A ghost chorus recited:
Two boys went to the penny arcade. With hands full of nickels.
Nudie one minutes nudie movie machines that clicked like a typewriter as the movie played. With hands full of nickels.

Peep show naughty strip poker stripers did tickle naughty naughty, just for a nickel.
Boy dreams with 1930s carnival girls with hot cotton candy and hot, hot dogs, long with the alphabet written in mustard.
Wash your hands before you eat.
Be on the lookout to not get caught.
But caught again, red handed.
Hand in the cookie jar of wishes and hopes and Ruby the fortune teller saw into a future of pipe dream burlesque and up set love.
With their nickels gone no more nickels of Duck Pond. Duckpondless lost nickels in eternity put the last nickel in the collection, basket, of forever, remember.

The *Buffalo Evening News* reported that: seven Buffalo teens escaped uninjured in a collision of two cars on the Laff in the Dark ride at Crystal Beach. When the two cars collided, a wire shorted out, sparks flew over the cars, and hit the ceiling and the ride filled with smoke. It looked like real ghosts were rising from their graves. They felt lucky to have gotten out. Firefighters were called to the scene. Crystal Beach Manager Ruby the Tart, a fortune teller, noted that apparently a car came off the rail and a wire in the floor shorted out causing some insulation to burn. There was a feeling of burning, inside, everyone. Ruby said: the rail is electrified but grounded, and there was no danger of electrocution. Park management offered free passes to the seven teens involved but was turned down: dah, ass wipe, cause they being fucking scared to death of ghosts!

The Magic Palace was a walk-through funhouse with distortion mirrors, tilting room, air blowers, tipping wall, bar maze, and slide. The mirrors stretched her into new forms, made him fatter, shorter, her face distorted, massaged her face into a monster, into his real face, into a forest creature, a blossom, into the Minotaur, into Aphrodite, into Marilyn Monroe, into her pliable ghost. Ruby sat in the funhouse reading fortunes between one and three. She wore a turban and saw him in her crystal ball. His future was in the mirrors. Her future was in the tilting room.
She laughed when straw came out of his ears.

Still early on a Lake Erie dawn morning about June 10:30 AM rosy fingers spread apart, peanut butter spreads easily, a teenage girl was thrown fresh from the Wild Mouse at Crystal Beach Amusement Park. There was a strange fragrance in the air.

The Memorial Rose Petals© Sorrowful White are beautiful white to ivory petals in color, which are a perfect color for anyone as they are pure in sorrowful mourning. They, pulled and freeze dried to last up to about two months. They, look and feel like fresh petals for weeks, where normal petals would start to brown in a day or two. They, offer a strange smell, an artificial smell, almost plastic like a plastic botanical garden in an aerosol can for a funeral parlor.

Down, she fell 25 feet down and suffered a massive head injury. One witness said she lost her head. Folk heard her say: I leave my head. Someone heard her say: where's my spacecraft, take me to my spacecraft. Her High Quality and Low-Price Rhinestone Pageant Tiara was found undamaged.

Her ghost said: if you were there I would go in the bushes with you. They would be in the bushes forever if he were there.
Did you see the departed in the small cluster of shrubs sometimes suggesting a thick, shaggy patch of hair?
She heard an unknown music, indescribable, from under his seat, and she returned to her saucer shaped ship. It was black and white. It left, with her. She left it, with him. I could only dream of her. Dream on sucker. But you never know. Don't rock the spaceship of hope. Don't make waves, radiation. If you see a ghost, don't tell nobody. Nobody will believe nothing you write, and they, will hate you, forever.

At Crystal Beach there were many reports of UFOs suddenly appearing in the sky from nowhere and then disappearing, seemingly in an instant. They, were a circle shape. They, were a red round light that turned green. They, were like eggs frying in the sky. Jack Fay, a retired captain with the New York State Police who now works as a MUFON field investigator, said the sightings were made by very credible people. MUFON means: The Mutual UFO Network.

Loki's name would seem to mean knot or tangle. Freyja was asleep in a Crystal Beach cabin. Freya's room was sealed while she slept, so Loki turned himself into a fly to enter through unseen gaps. Freyja was wearing her necklace while sleeping. Once Freyja turned over, the necklace's clasp was exposed, and Loki was able to unfasten and remove it from Freyja's neck. Loki collected the necklace after picking up a yellow duck with the number 67 on the bottom.

Her ghost said: I became your sucrose ghost searching for red lipstick, for wet mascara. I touch your dark, inferior place. I need your pink matrimony, lipstick, or I will die, without makeup.
She died. She got stuck on the ride when his chain broke. She panicked and fell, for him, hard, as they say.

Her ghost said: my pathological immaterial kiss kisses your sweetspot's molecular formula: $C12H22O11$, sugar, $C12H22O11$, is an organic compound, sugar, sucrose, is a carbohydrate, it is a disaccharide composed of one glucose, $C6H12O6$, and one fructose, $C6H12O6$, unit, drosophila, is a genus of flies, belonging to the family Drosophilidae, whose members are often called fruit flies or wine flies, a reference to the characteristic of many species to linger around overripe fruit for the fermenting sugars.
♪ Sugar, ah honey honey.
Her ghost said: I can change, for you, from an elephant into a ghost, into a fly.

The next Friday, his ghost sat in a diner, a Deco, by the Genesee bus turnaround. His brain hoovered around: Eggs of the poetry of the cosmos! Cook my alien eggs in metallic egg circles! Eggs, in a one ear and out the other! Eggs circle the Egyptian lettuce mummified and fried Nile! Locked, he kept thinking of sorrowful breakfast, a meal without punishment or Penance, pancakes. Just as his ghost slipped into the Deco, a fly also flew into the Deco. He now bears the head of a fly. His atoms have become mixed up with the fly, and now he is unable to reverse the procedure. Deciding that his transmitter will be a bogy rather than a blessing to humankind, he smashed the apparatus and burned his poems. He then instructed her, via body language, to crush his fly like head and hand. Her ghost gave him her hand, in. And then while staring intently at a spider's web in the garden, she saw a tiny entrapped fly tinnily screaming: Help me! Help me! as her salivating spider approached him. She hesitates and, squish squash, mooush, oh well, life goes on. Her falsies floating in her inground pool at dawn.

Her ghost said: at first, I didn't think this would be a good mascara, but I actually really like this! I wouldn`t say that it really makes my natural eyelashes looks like falsies, but I still love it, this mascara definitely thickens my natural lashes and it also lengthens them, but I don`t think to an extreme point, as for the mascara wand, it is flat yet curved like a scimitar or the moon.

His ghost was reading the newspaper in the Deco no. 6 by Walden and Bailey about this guy who lost his eye at Crystal Beach. He remembered that Odin had one eye. When Odin arrived at Mimir's well, he asked Mimir for a drink of loganberry. Mimir knew how yummy loganberry and vodka was and refused unless Odin offered an eye in return.
Odin said: Oh well, what the fuck.
He gouged out one of his eyes and dropped it in like an egg into a hot, frying pan.
Bill Healy was blind in one eye.
Robert Creeley lost an eye as a child.
My eyes popped out of my head.
Up to my eyeballs.
Twinkle.
Keep an eye out.
Odin was the god of poetry and ecstasy.
Odin's crows were thought and memory.
His ghost thought that poetry would be enough:
Now that you're a ghost
You're like a slice of toast

His ghost said: O condemned to haiku:

noodle knob magnet window
refrigerator
pill face pen flying teacups

And then his ghost wroted:

Crystal Beach Limerick:

Ferris cyclone will ticket tomato
Fun boomerang eggshell tomorrow
      Glove skeleton laugh
      Corn beef pine tree
Pirate snow pizza avocadoes

His ghost said: I am not sure, of anything, but I think the ghost said: tub bunny.
Her ghost said: your nuts? you listen to too much Bob Dylan.

The Endtipity of this Serpentine Tale

His ghost said: it was his endless love song tail to her wrapping around her finger like a plucked loose thread, dental floss.
Her ghost said: wishful thinking.
His ghost said: I only wrote it for you only like a doctor appointment.
Her ghost said: I don't get it? this is supposed to be about me?
She didn't understand how diptera and fungus gnats were about her.
Her ghost said: it's pretty short, a pretty shitty little poem, could you spare it?
Guilty, he incanted a ghost poem to her ghost: raised off by leaves and black ear free coffee, from Costa Rica, pear beached lipped lap dance against, the eyes of salt white butter melt, water lliquefied by liquor lacquer, flies of fly parts, on the tips of overheard grass and/or kiss on the nipple tips, dick tips, tips opposition to, onto, of, on top, of it, top it off, the wheel of closing, his eyes, listen up, let me give you a tip.
The wheel of zipping his fly.
Guilty diptera and fungus gnat eggs.
Slowly each day thereafter he became crazier, slipped into insanity. I plead guilty. I plead insanity. I stayed in his room forever, where he was safe to repeat the cycle: because ghosts sleep on him, laid, sticky side up, sailing to Egypt. Elephantine lust makes me happy. You? Larva? Luxor towels and the morning after a good dream when she would love him forever in the unreal world of his own bed to lie in it, unnatural, at least a shadow, at last my levitating red lava lamp.
His ghost informs with a spell charm delight in drink for clarity was everywhere an incant: white as sea ice and sane whose eyes hose and feed L'Oreal on root hairs.
Invoke: Clairol. L'Oréal. Clairol. L'Oréal.
Owl fell out the shadow's tit.
Her dream cast a shade of sparrows.
Surrendering to the moon he became the night enemy of the holy hot July sun.
The sun tortures him on the naked paper rack, imprisons him, in her patriotism, in the stiff rigidity of light moving only in a guilty straight line.
This is nuts.
Shadows are not something.

I really don't know why the bean bag chair was floating up near the ceiling.
Ghosts don't really exist. Do they?
I know you don't believe me but I found her shadow in the living room.
I don't believe you!
Please, pretend this didn't happen.
Say the dog knocked over the plants.
It was an accident.
It's not my shadow.
No one will believe this but shadows broke all the beer bottles in the basement and then grabbed hold my elbow.
Don't tell anyone!
It was really cold.
I know this sounds crazy but I heard: Clairol. L'Oreal. Clairol. L'Oreal.

Intermissions at the Broadway Drive-In

A Melody

♪ When I was a sailor lad
♪ I had a pot of gold
♪ I pissed away my gold
♪ I pissed away my gold

♪ When I was a youngish pig
♪ I drank up all the booze
♪ I pissed away my time
♪ I pissed away my time

♪ When I was a poet toad
♪ I loved a tartly tart
♪ I pissed away her dreams
♪ I pissed away my dreams

Concession Stand

His ghost said: Buffalo poetry history offers us a magical potion of stories and practices infused with charms, cramps, herbs, and superstition. it started with bread made, in large part, with rye, and rye and rye-like plants can host ergot, a powerful hallucinogen. records from the 14th to the 17th century mention the Polish affliction with dancing mania, which found groups of people dancing through streets, often speaking nonsense and foaming at the mouth.
Puree reach peach pus- Ponce de Leon.
Puss puch paczki- Ponce de Leon.
Ponch ouch.
This can be genetic.
Ancestry.com.
Ergotism egotism.
When a black cath
Crossed her path
And a bird poops on his head

She will be rich
So, check my plumbing…
There seems to be a cloddy glitch
Son-of-a-bitch.
To bind another to his delight.
Her ghost said: just blow it out your ass!
Genes transmit his moods… see also those who experienced him, his mania would later accumulate into wild visions that she accompanied, her lips, he being a being whose biological progenitors crashed to earth, in Buffalo, in the long snow.
His ghost pushed her dry clean only clothes into the washer on hot.
Her ghost made sure she got some Ivory soap into the open tip of his dick.
Her ghost said: he acts like he has a horseshoe up his ass.
His ghost busted alota mirrors.
    The Mirror Shards
Grind them up
Put'em in a cup
With a little beer
For good luck
Bottoms up.
He belonged nowhere, and they chased him into the forest, carrying torches and screaming, and singing Beach Boy songs about surfing, cars, and hamburger stands.
    ♪ Help me Ronda. Help, help me Ronda.

A Cartoon

Common toads from the genus Bufo produce hallucinogens called bufotoxins. He looked at her toad and saw her two conspicuous bumps, located close to her ears. These were her parotid glands. She thought, and they produce his bufotoxins. He squeezed them for a long while and a foamy whitish stuff secreted. That's a bitter pill. That's hard to swallow. Pride gone. She was a tough Nut. Down the hatch. Tuesday is the best day for initiating mad honey hunting. Do not sip hallucinogenic Nepali red honey on the 8th, 11th, 23rd, 26th, and 30th day of the Hekt moon cycle. In small doses her mad honey can ensure a soothing sense

of inebriation. He swallowed whatever I said, hook, line, and sinker. In larger quantities, he can induce cardiac arrest, full-scale hallucinations or a period of time when the body seems to undergo a purge.
You haveta stop it! right Now.
I hop you can stop, that.
Stop what you're doin.
Impure vowels.
Hypnotic spellings.
Jingling jiggling keys that make the past lives live again.
The hope moon set.
"Abandon hoop all ye who enter, here."
Hoop-De-Doo.
You got hops.
Imhotep.
Hopalong Cassidy.
Hoped up on pot.
Hoopla.
The nuns had him hop on an assembly line belt where he was chopped to pieces in a huge machine and reassembled as a good child.
♫ Bah-bah-bah-bah, bah-bah-bah-bah at the hop!

Short Subject: [Presenting Bufotoxins]

He felt always like he was being watched, there was always a nun with a ruler, there was always something he did wrong, something to confess, and he was being judged on the technical aspects of his French kissing her and his, being a troll, his uncontrollable groping. Such is his nature of his being haunted. He could see things in the dark, and he was tongue tied. At his feet, his stones, bezoars, his feathers from Pegasus, they were delivered by spirits, what the demons had in his mind for him, like the heart is the shape of a fist, brain food is a sea monster, the heart shape is a brothel, the brain sits in a brain cavity, cavity, the brain is the size of a healthy North American common toad, the heart is the size of a healthy North American common toad, one-half of the world's approximately 7,500 known amphibian species could go extinct in our lifetime.
The literary magazine wanted new, fresh, and innovative poetry, so he wrote:

Bufo
Beaufo
Tit fill
Hort
Ba (a silent letter of your choice) th.
  (be silent for a bit before reading the next line).
Her ghost pronounced: his poetry is a plague of fucking frogs!
But for bufotoxins, I could have owned a Starbucks or fixed toasters or turned the lights on and off. But what do you want me to do? But it's always been like this: toads with internal fecundation, all tadpole ghosts swimming about his skull, screaming, screeching, popping up at strange times like when he was riding the bus downtown, on Sunday!
Her ghost said: don't have a shit hemorrhage.

Coming Attractions

Her ghost said: I am a craving creature who walks thought time with him alone and only swallows venomous snakes, giant millipedes, scorpions, finches, and even bullfrogs, and a baker's dozen of sorrowful Hungarian violins whinging.
Bufotoxins: his ape-shit ghost confessed repeatedly without absolution. Possessed by ghosts, he appeared ridiculousness, a six pack of half-truth lies.
Her ghost said: you ruined me. a city known as Sais or Zau. go on a date me back to 3,000 B.C. I am a nasty cult, center, of creation and passion, and war. I am the location of the grave of Osiris, the fantasy afterlife. as Wadjet, the Cobra Goddess with her body coils of a glossy woman with the head of a devouring lion, yet, a host placed on his tongue, a witch he could not touch with his Yeti teeth.
She appeared at the summer solstice at the Villa Maria lawn fate, beneath the mature cottonwoods on the grounds of the Villa Maria complex at 600 Doat Street, built in 1929 by the Sisters of St. Felix, in Cheektowaga, in the beer tent, draft Iroquois beer, large cups for a buck.
Her ghost said: you fuckin ruined everything. what are you trying to pull??
His ghost said: the secret of immortality and my communion with the spirit world and self-transcendence.
His ghost said: it is because I drank toad fungus. they did it in Sais. they

did it in Atlantis. Shelley did it!
His ghost got up ona bench and spewed:
Toaster of toad toxins
Toe of frog
Smoked like hash
Do purrrrrrrrrrr* (*a word of variable spelling)
To nurrrvous disfunction
Victim twisting
San Cook sang: ♪ Twistin the night away
Caught in a tongue twister
Don't get your tit in the ringer
Ring out that wet dream
Bring out the ol' Vaseline! OOO-Ahhhhhhhhhh....
Her ghost opened his three-ring poem binder he labeled *Follies Brassiere*, and he felt purpling of the face, a tight feeling in the chest, prickling as if he were jabbed by a ghost with sewing needles, and he saw swirling, colored patterns typical of tryptamines, tending toward the arabesque.

Trailer from *Follies Brassiere*.

She recited from the poetry of *Follies*:

Winter in Buffalo by Michael Basinski

Minds as well write
About snow
In Buffalo
Even rhymes
And winter happens
In every heart
Stand out by Lake Erie
In Hauk's parking lot
When a Canadian wind witch starts whippin around
Dominatrix crosses the frozen lake
Chief weather anchor Kevin O'Connell said:
"It's an Alberta clipper."
You better have your zipper
Up

Paul Cezanne Said: The Day is Coming When a Single Carrot, Freshly Observed, Will Set-off a Revolution

My birth year? 1950 in November.
His ghost said: *The Thing from Another World* takes place on November 2 and 3, 1950. Buffalo firefighters said they had radio issues on the fire ground. Also, water quickly froze making walking tricky. Buffalo firefighters said they had radio issues on the fire ground. Also, water quickly froze making walking tricky.
Jack Kerouac married Joan Haverty on November 18, 1950.
The Carrot Gang was infamous in Buffalo during the 1950s.
In November 1950, troops of the 7th infantry division of the US Army's X-Corps became the first American division to reach the Yalu River.
American scientist heroes and American Air Force officials fend off a bloodthirsty vegetable-like alien organism while at a remote arctic outpost.
An American scientist called the Thing an intelligent carrot.
The average annual snowfall in Buffalo, New York is 93.4 inches.
A ghost said: she knows he is just using her.
He uses his magnifying glass to burn his captured water nymphs, ants, and grasshoppers.
The Thing was destroyed by flame thrower.
Her ghost said: he's a little strange, crazy, but he is pretty.
Her mother's ghost said: he's a bad apple.
Salivate over my jealousy and find what gourmets consider a buttery treat.
Her ghost said: apply the red pagan blush of the apple center to her cheeks.
Guilty, she was burned at the stake on 30 May 1431, dying at about nineteen years of age.
Hypatia's astronomy and mathematics led to suspicion of sorcery, and she was flayed alive by a mob of monks and her body burned.
He was the carrot in her eye.
His ghost said: broke your heart, cut you like an apple, horizontally, and find her star of Aphrodite.
Certain fruits and vegetables seem to have a self-destruct switch, the moment the knife pierces his skin, he set about destroying himself.

The scientists said: this is no dream; this is really happening.

His ghost said: a ghost which can assume the shape, memories, and personality of any living thing, and unliving, or even living room furniture.

A graceful covered bridge in Wyoming County, New York, east of Cowlesville over the Cayuga Creek, built in 1874, was 81 feet in length. In the late 1960s the bridge was lost to arson.

Great balls of fire.

Robinson Jeffers wrote, "Pleasure is the carrot dangled to lead the ass to market."

His ghost said: I'm goin to take a piss in those bushes.

Her ghost said: better take a magnifying glass.

j

A 50 50 Chance

Jack Bruce, drummer Ginger Baker, and guitarist/singer Eric Clapton.
♪ In the white room with black curtains near the station.
Half my life is over, his ghost said: I'm pissing blood.
Ghosty me said: That depends, is the bottle half full or half empty?
The time required for one half the atoms of a given amount of a radioactive substance to disintegrate could be a long time, around Christmas.
A slice of apple pie served in Deco no. 6, Walden Ave. and Bailey, at the counter.
Apple, with cinnamoom! Radium! Barium!
His ghost had coffee with Half n Half.
Half-and-half is a simple blend of equal parts whole milk and light cream.
Half & Half averages 10 to 12% fat, which is more than milk but less than light cream.
Due to its lower fat content than cream, it can't be whipped.
Her ghost wondered: could she get pregnant if he only put it in halfway?

K

More Others of the Other Ghost Tales

A

A Prelude

Can you remember the first poem you remember?
One day Phillip Morris got on his Camel to go see Chesterfield
On the way he found some Old Gold
Wasn't that a Lucky Strike?

A Preparation

Rule one for poets is that most people think poems to be a ridiculous pursuit.
Choose one of the following: (A) Prove them right (B) Be ridiculous (C) Most people?
This poem begins with a chorus of ghosts singing:
Choose one of the following: (A) "Little Drummer Boy" (B) "My Friend the Witch Doctor" (C) "Row Row Row Your Boat"
Begin.
All of you hear her ghost's soft chatter from a can of tuna, Chicken of the Sea (Albacore) in water (listen) from the grocery bag in the back seat:

> oorrphph
> aallaa
> uuee
> oppo
> oppo
> eeeeceee.

Scene - Carthage: Thee execution of Perpetua took place at the Circus, that is, in the public arena, for the entertainment of Governor Hilarian and the city of Carthage. It was his birthday and, on this special occasion, something special was offered to him. Perpetua rode in on an African elephant in her sassy ring master outfit, glittering, gold and blue, and was gracious, compromising, and willing to do anything she shouldn't be doing from her deep form, from pointed white pine forests, needles, barely visible in a sheer white sheet with cut out eyeholes, the night sky at night.

Her ghost said: once upon a time, in 1933....

Scene - Skull Island: only a dot on her ocean map 12°S 78°E, somewhere off the coast of Sumatra. There is a distinctive rocky knoll in the center of the island that is shaped like a human skull. A particular form of oyster, the Tahitian black lipped Pinctada margaritifera, which produces a black pearl, exists in thought, in huge oyster beds, all about the island, a circle, a noose placed over his memory.

A fascinating part of Japanese culture is that of the Ama pearl divers. Ama literally means woman of the sea, and she is recorded as early at 750 Anno Domini in the oldest Japanese anthology of poetry. These women specialize in freediving some 30 feet down into cold water wearing nothing.

Sea ghost she showed him the ring in the window of Glickstein's Jewelry at the Thruway Plaza.

His ghost said: I read her "Ode to a Skylark", she wished a black, pearl future and furniture from F & W Furniture Warehouse (FREE DILIVERY). You wanted I wasn't.

Promises where a secret kept is worth a thousand words.

Here nickname was Monster.

Keeping a secret can lead to depression, anxiety, poor overall health, and art and peotry, and alcoholism, and drug dependency.

Her ghost said: I had time to read the small print, an open book.

I stood there and forever sucked on my secrets until they melted like tart lemon, yellow hard candy in hot saliva, and again and again returned like Prometheus's liver.

I was an ice cube in her saliva.

Her ghost said: you're a waste of time.

His ghost said: I got plenty of time.

She wasted my time, so I got wasted on Almaden hearty burgundy.

His ghost said: I didn't waste time.

Almaden (Amlodipine besylate) is a dihydropyridine derivative.

Almaden frequently causes dizziness, headache, and somnolence, and often hypertonia, hypoaesthesia/paraesthesia, peripheral neuropathy, tremor, insomnia, and mood changes.

Freddy Fender sang: ♪ Wasted days and wasted nights.

B

Olson and Electra

Scene: Morning, again, ghost cries from his Serta perfect sleeper: ⇆⇶ᄃ˄˷!
Charles Olson said: north of Route 20 in Buffalo, in Batavia, it's the Devonian.
Ghost chorus:
>Trilobite!
>Brachiopods!
>Crinoids!
>Cephalopods!
>Bryozoan!
>Rugose!
>Gastropods!

350 million years ago the Devonian is also known as the Age of Fishes, since several major fish lineages evolved at this time. Sea levels were high, and the global climate was warm. The sea surface temp was 86 degrees Fahrenheit.
>Long time no sea.
>Washed out to sea.
>Three sheets to the wind.
>Walk the plank.
>Long time no sea.

You can fossil hunt for Devonian fossils, south of Buffalo, on Hamburg Beach.
>On Hamburg Beach, I have time to spend.
>Do you have time to kill?

Turn on the radio.
♪ I will follow him (follow him), follow him wherever he may go.
His ghost said: just say the magic word.
Her ghost said: abracadabra.
His ghost said: I will be with you forever, like a scar.
♪ The mountain's high
♪ And the valley's so deep,
♪ Can't get across

♪ To the other si-hi-hi-hi-hi-hi-hi-hi-hide.
Time's up.
Swimming in cut off shorts.
Electra plotted revenge.
We walked slowly across the street.
The Buick Electra is a full-size luxury car that was built by Buick from 1959 to 1990.
Her ghost said: in your dreams, sweetheart.
Time out.
A ghost wailed.
A ghost yowled.
A car horn blared.
His ghost shouted: horn blows, do you?

C

The consonants have been removed to protect the identity of the ghosts involved.
Chant: e o o a a e e e e o e o o e e i e i o e o i o e

His ghost sang: ♫ Walking down Walden cock in my hand
♫ I'm a mean mother fucker
♫ I'm an eastside man
His ghost pondered why this poem was in his head along with French toast?
Walking down Walden, entering the doomed city of Ilium, he heard something murmur mumble from his forever of frozen time.
A tree ghost chattered from a witch's bush: O! darkling, neither here nor there, when you are there and then, she also then, here, and there, nether, there in the Tarzan movie quicksand scene sinking secret July, the silent forever muse cursed, you:
Ac waba ind ut
Yaj baka yaj baka
Vot voko vot viko fatark.
His ghost had an image of a perfect three foot trophy poem.
Like a poem that defines all that was ever important to everybody, a poem in all the important immortal anthologies.
Her ghost a survivor.
Her ghost a carnival souvenir, stuffed, yellow and pink, a huge immoral cartoon like dog ready for Goodwill.
His ghost said: once upon a time? you think so? really? do you really think so? I don't think so, never, NEV-VER, EV-VER.
Her ghost incanted: mirrors cleaned with white linen, nude in a tub of sea salted water.
Cast: His head will turn my way.
Light three white tea candles.
Light with a wooden match two pink and one blue, one green, one red, and one yellow tea candles.
Cast: His head will turn my way.
Turn the lights low and begin playing Alice Coltrane records.
Cast: His head will turn my way.

Be saucy and reckless with yourself.
Cast: His head will turn my way.
Breathe deeply and wash with a hungry washcloth.
Cast: His head will turn my way.
Begin to relax.
Cast: I am loving, I am loved and love myself.
Cast: His head will turn my way.
Be one with incense, bath oils and herbal extracts of all sort.
In mind all ways the target of your spell.
Stoke the fire of each candle.
Stroke.Stroke.
Cast: I am loved.
Cast: And his head turns my way forever.
Remember that it is best to not blow the candles out but rather let them diminish on their own.
If they wi (sh) (ll)
If he will.
Mimba moomba flimma mur
Pleek wa feek han oop yalore.

D

The vowels are removed to protect the identity of the ghosts at the Broadway Drive-in.
Chant: t h v w l r l r l m l v l d l t l p r t c t t h d n t t y f t h g h s t t t h b r d w y d r v

Her ghost said: what they want is for you to carve beauty from hell.
She has a screw loose.
She bites.
If you screw around with him.
Screw you.
He'll screw you and leave.
She screwed me.
Play with fire.
His uroboro bruises upon her neck and thigh not a spiraling off of or I do.
Skimpy in intense sunlight.
A tornado sucking a beautiful red balloon, deflated.
The act of turning a suckling pig in a passion pit, pearls before.
Or having a loose thread.
Screwed or sewed a pearl.
Here, drink this purple passion.
Bibbellee bobbily book.
Stinging graveyard nettles to knit into a shirt to help him regain his human shape.
To screw him this is what you wanted him to do all along.
To you and she gave a hurt blaze.
A witch's kiss you fuzzy little dog.
A hoop, on fire, now jump without hope.

An Intermission

A Ghost Nocturn

Feeling a hand or something brush, the past, or push or nudge or knead, scratching.
Chant:
Imbolc Imbolc in the belly
Time to return to Percy Bryce Shelley.
I pulled out your breast from the scant cobwebs.
Hexes nest way up in the cottonwoods.
Her ghost said: and July ghosty as white bread toasted with too much butter, real butter, melting icebergs of, and apple jelly swimming in it without my bathing suit.
Investigated his pan burning the moon whites of my eyes. Pop.
Jack Kerouac wrote, "…and my whole life was a haunted life, the life of a ghost."
This dancing night dripped of unimportant white washcloths, wrung.
Greasy treats used them to mascara.
The form of the old man faded for he would not partake of her morning sun.
♪ The light turned green, you know what I mean, ba,ba,ba,ba, deep in the heart of Texas.
Her voile ghost said: ba,ba,ba,ba, into thin air.

i

Everyday

A neutrino is a lepton, an elementary particle with half-integer spin, that interacts only via the weak subatomic force and gravity.
Physicists call the neutrino the ghost particle.
Buddy Holy's ghost sang:
♪ Every day, it's a-gettin' closer
♪ Goin' faster than a roller coaster
♪ A-hey, a-hey hey.
Allen Ginsberg wrote, "The tongue and cock and hand and asshole holy."
Holly can prevent lightning strikes.
His ghost told his buddy Al: it was like being truck-struck by a lightning bolt.
Emily Dickinson wrote, "Lightning is a yellow fork."
William Burroughs wrote, "a frozen moment when everyone sees what is on the end of every fork."
His friend Larry's ghost said: fork off!
Lightning bugs use bioluminescence during warm June twilight to attract mates, or prey.
His smitten ghost wrote: lightning undressed as a ripe red tomato with eye holes!
Neutrinos are denoted by the Greek letter V.
The letter V appears in Venus, involved, and Road Vultures (as in R.V.M.C. the Road Vultures Motorcycle Club).
The letter V is mysterious and holy and erotic and has a magical significance.
Her ghost said: if you rub yourself with the letter V, you, well, I can't be responsible.
His endless ghost was in thrall and exchanged his shape in a region some called Cheektowaga, New York, an island.
No ghost is an island.
On June 18, 2014 on Alcatraz a woman snapped a photo of a ghost that authorities refused to authenticate.
Ghosts blow household fuses and lightbulbs.
Her ghost was dressed as a nocturnal snow drift.

Her ghost was a cutout eye of lightning in a round, red, fire cloud or an obscure, worm eaten manuscript from the Middle Ages.

Her ghost said: if you are here and are not here then you are there.

Supernatural objects appear on stage: a wreath of her hair, his ears were elves, the waterfall sounded like the speech of dark birds.

When the phone rings, it's a ghost.

Neutrinos oscillate between different flavors in flight mostedly often strawberry, chocolate, and French vanilla.

French vanilla uses a custard base whereas vanilla is a regular cream based ice cream.

French kissing stimulates endorphin release and reduces acute stress levels.

Her ghost said: do not harm the stones by stepping on her, toes.

His ghost was unidentified but refused the mixed drink of forgetfulness.

Thus, neutrinos typically pass through normal matter unimpeded and undetected.

j

A July Ghost Tale

D. H. Lawrence wrote, "Like a ghost he came, through the drizzling rain. And like a ghost he saw her sitting, waiting in the porch of the hut." Suzerain of Weather for Channel 7, Autumn Lewandowski said: The storms could bring hail and high, damaging winds strong enough to take down trees, and the line of storms could dump up to an inch of rain. By noon they should dissolve, be, all but gone.
I see things that are not there.
Her ghost said: after the alphabet, aftershock.
His ghost said: you'll never be gone for good.
He repeated, second grade. He was trained, early. He ate, paste.
A ghost was in the wet air with a white wet clingy top.
Her ghost said: you know who I am, I know you know who I am, I know you know I am you.
Peak winds could be 50 mph.
Sneak a peek.
Take a peek.
Peek inside.
No peeking.
Piqued your interest.
Don't peek.
You wish.
It was July again.
In conversation she said: I am always hearing ghosts. And swatted at the air in front of her face as if bombarded by a flock of lusting fruit flies.
Fruit flies are built to find fermenting, rotting fruit.
The female fly pierces the fruit with her sharp ovipositor and inserts a single egg just below the skin, leaving a small scar on the surface. The egg is creamy white, about 0.6 mm (.02 in.) long, and slightly curved.
In the ripe, rabid, humid, heat of July, cherry season lasts about 10 days, and sayonara.
Her ghost said: there was no edge, no end, just an opening.
In July, lawn fetes around Buffalo are one almost every summer weekend at a Catholic Church some place like Corpus Christi or Transfiguration.

The Villa Maria lawn fate was when summer was about to rage. Lawn fates have polka bands in the beer tent with one dollar huge cups of Iroquois draft beer and gambling games, spinning wheels of fortune, and:
♪ Ja cie kocham, ja cie lubie
♪ Ale nie dam az po slubie
♪ Oj Dana Dana oj Dana.
The player tosses a ping-pong ball onto a grid of small goldfish open goldfish bowls with little gold goldfish within. The object is to get a ball to drop into the goldfish bowl. If so, if the ball drops just so, you win the goldfish within. In the beer tent, little plastic bags each with a golden goldfish sat on the makeshift bar.
Her ghost said: you remain a goldfish.
In a smallish goldfish bowl.
A goldfish is carp.
The dead goldfish got flushed down the toilet.
Poof. Up in smoke.
Jack Kerouac wrote, "Take care of my ghost, ghost."

Five Intermittent Intermissions Tied into a Knot

1

Caught
It happened at the beginning of time
Down came her rain
And washed his spider out

Aside.
Her ghost chattered: this, your-poem-that-you-wrote-me, about me?
what has this to do about me? take-out, Ja-Fa-Fa Hots,
♪ Shelly brand meat products
♪ Really grand meat products
♪ Old fashion good
♪ by Szelagowski.
pull your pud, red hots,
♪ Don't give me that baloney, I want Wardynski's!
slice-a-cheese-pizza, it's the cops, leg of lamb, chops, tomato chips? he went looney tunes, and his head up his ass, up upon a pillow of pillows my ass his eye, apple of, *Candy*, Terry Southern, Milk Duds, what else can I do?
♪ Who stole the kishka?*
*Kishka is a type of fat and round and firmly packed ring sausage made from a combination of meat and meal stuffed into a sausage skin.
your oily hands, your pale pie hole goblin stuffed, passenger side hide, gremlin gnaw, Buick Skylark, ghost white, 1967, hitching a ride, my mother knows in profuse strains of unpremeditated art.
His ghost said: exaggerated simple images rather than real lines, with a pencil, bit off eraser, lead poisoning, constipation, irritability, memory problems, lack of original ideas, reliance on established forms, tingling in the hands, head.
Going to the movies: *2001 A Space Odyssey*, Century Theatre, 511 Main Street, opened in 1921, 3000 plus seats, trembling balcony empty now a Burger King, trippy.
Her ghost said: make it go away, mom.

HAL says he is foolproof and incapable or error.
Her ghost slurs: the-car-door-slammed upon-my-toes, jam, S-methyl thioesters, asparagus, shut off his water, urine, his gas, his Lammas no more, his Direct TV, his sparrow of sorrow.
Ann Darrow Ann Darrow full with sorrow.
King Kong dead King Kong dead King Kong dead.
ribbons weep upon his St. Francis fingertip, stain, a quiet swallowing puddle of saliva serves up a lubricative function, wetting food and permitting the initiation of swallowing, raccoon, and protecting the mucosal surfaces of the oral cavity from the desiccation of his kisses.
HAL said: I can see you're really upset about this. I honestly think you ought to sit down calmly, take a stress pill, and think things over.
Her ghost said: French movie, I predict the beauty of Frenches Mustard writing yellow on a footlong, experimental, hot dog.

♪ Daisy…
♪ Daisy…
♪ Give…
♪ me…
♪ yore…
♪ heart…
♪ to do…

2

Visitation Rights

In your bathroom I stole some loose hair from your hairbrush.
Hair: the specialized epidermal structure produced only by mammals, developing from a papilla sunk in the corium.
In the night, I set up a cup of water on the windowsill.
His pale ghost said: I have become white ashes, white.
Red is not a rose.
Wouldn't you know it, he had a nosebleed.
Ring-a-round the rosie, A pocket full of posies, Ashes! Ashes!, We all fall down.
Her ghost said: you do not remember me, you remember yourself.
He's just using her like any of the fine threadlike strands that sprout

sweet from the human skin.
While French kissing at the drive-in, she thought why use the alphabet, assassin, bind, I can read your mind.
In his ghost mind, utter:

ant a an
a an gift ov woo
as and uf dl nd af
Atropos....

Her witch sang: ♪ Ol' McDonald had a farm, e i e i o!
In his fantasy half-dream nighties of obey nighttime, almost real to feel, almost anytime, cyclops wishes warm Wendy, said: Peter, I bind your shadow to mine, shackle.
Let set on the windowsill forever all thee long night long forever and let the long inevitable spell of the reincarnated bind, sew-by-hand, toes mingle drink tingle, ♪ Jingle all the way.
♪ O what fun...
... to keep the heart beating
... once each night during the cycle of the full moon
... you will dissolve three tana leaves
... come morning download guzzle down
Mind in bind spell, drink this, forever, and ever.
Amen.

3

Blurb: Like Finding Your Zipper Open in Church

His ghost dropped a fork, which means a guest ghost will soon arrive soon.
Her ghost said: his misty eyes of Halloween moons Nix and Hydra! look at his hand, his fingers look like cucumbers, dick warts, walking under a ladder.
I saw a human form, black cat, suit, an apparition that looked like the planet Pluto, not a planet, Pluto does not speak, Arf!
You may also see her brightly colored orbs, or bit.
Her blue wispy orbs are often his spirits, and her white orbs are often her ghosts.

Scene: Gumball machine, squad car lights, like a night club, "In A Gadda Da Vida," reported on the evening news knows I attacked him with a kitchen knife like a wild pig crashing through the Białowieża Forest.
I need forgiveness.
And I will remember.
When I can't remember.
Anymore.
Her ghost said: I broke my compact mirror.
Seven years to be misty, transparent or solid, Penance, wink.
Her sleeping causes madness and ghosts bite you while you sleep.
If a ghost hits you between your eyes you will go blind.
Mists behave like human fingers in her movie, house, opening an umbrella, thirteenth floor, fingers leave no prints, curl.
His enchantment was believed to contain my comets, asteroids, and other small bodies made largely of her torn ice and my ice pieces, my sisters of scissors, and my sickness in Kleenex, saliva within your yore, lore, seems to be real evidence to support her idea that in such areas of powdery mist, live-in, living in sin, in the living room, ghosts.

4

Meander Drinking from a Green Garden Hose

The shape of a hose is cylindrical.
A hose is a flexible tube that carries water from one point to another.
Arty said his cock was a tube steak.
His ghost said: I'm fucked up, look at my hand, the hair keeps growing back.
Speaking slow and quietly but emphatically, her ghost uttered: most of the 21 hoses they tasted were made from polyvinyl chloride, a toxic plastic that often contains endocrine-disrupting stabilizers known as organotins, which can interfere with hormonal and reproductive development. more than half of the 21 hoses tasted contained matrimony, which, with prolonged exposure, can lead to kidney and liver damage, and about five percent contained bromine. both antimony and bromine are markers of flame retardants used in plastics.
His ghost said: I drunk my heart fireproof.

Asbestos is fire resistant.
Ghosts are the color of asbestos.
Long, thin, fibrous crystals with each fiber like a finger composed of millions of fibrils that reach and release by abrasion, skin flakes, flicks.
A ghost's finger can enter into a body via the mouth or other portal and ghost fingers can reach deep into the lungs deep.
Asbestos can cause lung cancer, mesothelioma and asbestosis, and many other diseases causing an extreme discomfort.
Exposure to ghosts causes intense discomfort.
Her ghost said: I can almost feel them around me, like little white lost wind feathers, plume, or little tingle fine little softy hair like bruising past me something touched me, in my the dark, plum.
Knocked my socks off, scared her socks off, pants, smile at her and her pants fall down, beat, bore, catch-charm, flyby, on the fly, zip-up, zippy, or the horse will get away, gone.
♪ Zip pa de do da.

5

R is for read more
"And I pluck'd a hallow reed"
And When You Hear that Song Again and Again, You See a Ghost.

A jukebox is a partially automated music-playing device, usually a coin-operated machine, 10 cents a song or 3 for a quarter, use-ta-be, that will play my selection from self-contained media. The classic jukebox has buttons with letters and numbers on them that, when entered in combination, are used to play a specific selection, like: R 6.
Abba sang: ♪ Knowing me, knowing you (a-ha).
Poets, if you combine the correct letter and number sounds, the love you lost will appear, second chance, by chance, another shot, a snowball in hell, fat chance, your chance of swallowing a ghost hole are a whole lot better.
And ghosts have chicken egg shaped eyes.
And they paint them black, black crow full skies.
And ghosts look like bed bobbing sheets about.
Her ghost said: up for grabs, choice is, and yours smells of sauerkraut.

And inside the sheet is empty.
And better than nothing.
Good, under the sheets.
Like the human heart or a sheet of paper, it's dark in here.
And get your hand in there dexterous.
The odor of gasoline and hoaxy lyrics.
And empty accepting the honeybees.
Honey Bee was a burlesque star, stripper, stripping.
And her little letters vibrating them bee ghosts waggle.
And his ghost said: (a-ha).

S A Musical

A forest ghost, creature like the damp, a white tree white frog sang, in a short high trill fog, a little more musical than a sea nymph standing in form in front of the microwave, foam. (chant:)

hyla / cinerea

polypedates / leucomystax / rhacophoridae

cochranella / pulverata / centrolenidae

leptopelis / vermiculatus / hyperoliidae

boophis / albilabris / mantellidae

pedostibes / tuberculosus / hyperoliidae

We found that female ability to discriminate attractive calls increased when several attractive call components were available, providing novel evidence that the use of multicomponent signals enhances communication in complex acoustic conditions. Signal discrimination in females also improved with speaker separation, demonstrating that within natural choruses, spatial unmasking conditioned by male density, and spatial separation probably improves female discrimination of competing males. (chant:)

hyla / cinerea

polypedates / leucomystax / rhacophoridae

cochranella / pulverata / centrolenidae

leptopelis / vermiculatus / hyperoliidae

boophis / albilabris / mantellidae

pedostibes / tuberculosus / hyperoliidae

Denny the Pope's ghost said: you never know, so, keep a rubber in your wallet.

Danny's ghost said: having a rubber on you is like sunscreen.

Coppertone's ad shows a young blond topless girl in pigtails staring in surprise as a Spaniel puppy sneaks up behind her and pulls down her blue swimsuit bottom showing her ass to be lighter than the rest of her body.

Danny's ghost said: don't be a paleface.

Disney's Pluto said: Arf!

Denny the Pope went into Vincie's Drugstore and said: gimme a three pack of Trojans,, please.

My own rubber owned like having the Holy Ghost in a tiny square package, I believed, agnostic.

Her ghost said: touch what you should not touch
Touch that which is not here: her ghost said.
(Now, enter this poem like a frog or common North American toad and croak or cluck or make a high-pitched trill (for 30 seconds or more), bellow, play the banjo, squeak, groan, chirp - long or short or in bursts, variable pitch from low or high. Improvise and orchestrate).
X-Ray Specs were long advertised with the slogan: See the bones in your hand, see through clothes! Some versions of the advertisement featured an illustration of a young man using the X-Ray Specs to examine the bones in his hand while a voluptuous woman stood in the background, as though awaiting her turn to be X-rayed, his tongue was out, dripping tongue sweat.
In his sweet head while a voluptuous woman stood wet in the background and looked him directly in the eyes, his body produces a chemical called phenylethylamine, no strange hand might touch him, no strange eye may look through his thin, milk sheer, rayon white of words their bones black.
Must be nice.

      uucills
      mmiioo
      seeeeb
      ribbit

A j

Her ghost said: I can read the poem inside his head and it's better than on the page, sheer, you're mind goes on forever, O no!
He jacked-off, her shadowless being drifted across Walden Avenue into the night up Haller Street, thin, thread, binding her yellow hair, way down to over by Shit's Creek, necking, six minutes.
For him she the math goddess who holds all the corners of a circle, open, with her finger clips.

>   thumb
>   the index finger
>   the middle finger
>   the ring finger (on left hand only)
>   the pinkie finger
>   thumb

A thin sheet of cloth you might see through him or see her being a binge sea.
Is that a banana in your pocket or am I seeing a ghost, a moth, the sunlight, a stop sign, a Swiss cheese sandwich on Vienna bread?
She haunts him and when she enters your you, enter.
Her haunts you her melted candy bar on the passenger seat.
Your deep blue and yellow petunias, your oil change, and all the wind of all the garbage days, garbage cans going rolling everywhere, possessed.
Free of all the time there ever is on every finger in every pie, count them.
Keep your fingers crossed and your friends closer.
He fingered her and secretly smelled the sweet violets, recorded by Mitch Miller and Dinah Shore, ♪ See the USA in your Chevrolet, America is asking you to call, pulled out a plum.
Her ghost gave him the innuendo finger as she walked out to the waiting yellow cab, never wrote back, that's all she wrote.
♪ Don't ya love her as she's walkin out the door.
She was, and you have all her time in eternity.
And otherworldly to haunt her as she hunts you down, daily.
Your shadow among a forest of shadows, obvious, apparent, distinct, disconnected, absorbed, as to be nothing at all, dried clear, see thought, sheared.

She shut off the light in the basement, by the wash tubs, washing machine, Maytag.
Of lost shadows under the cushions of the coach were levitating objects, coins, pens, Bobby Pins, peanut shells, the TV remote.
Misplacing his keys is indicative of her ghost oozing with negative energy.
She had him wrapped around her finger.
Wrapping at his chamber door.

K again

K Again Prelude

His ghost said: can you remember the first poem you remember?
A little bird
With a yellow bill
Sat upon my windowsill
I lured him in
With a slice of bread
And then I smashed
His fuckin head

Prelude

People sometimes report that areas of dense sound are ghosts, like an area of dense sound using the letter D words like: dale dude drown dork.

> Dizzy dry dry die
> Daft dewy
> Detour deconstruction
> Dizzy dry, up,
> Drip.

Preparation

His ghost was so in love with her a sparrow sat on the finger of her cat. The Benu bird portrayed as a long-legged, wading heron in the moon temple of Cheektowaga, Walden Ave. and Harlem Road, created his otherworldly cosmos, and made beings of gods and goddesses to live in her made universe.
♪ Well everybody know that the bird is a word
♪ Com ma mau papa com-a mau

1

> Doctor doctor dildo doctor
> Dizzy dew double D
> Dickcompose disappear
> Disappointment did-m-doggy
> Dumb done
> Done dumb
> Different doddle dildo dip.

Her ghost said: the phone rings from his former fingers, Dial, soap up his cock, KY, soap-on-a-rope, soap opera, it will all come out in the wash, wash his poem out, with soap, wash out his crooked mind, soft-soap, soap him up, hay - no soap, rejection letter.
Her ghost said: you and me, all I gotta say is don't drop the soap.
His ghost said: I am not looking back, I am looking out, at your finger prints all over my glasses, tips, TV, window at your obvious forest fire, on which deer, witch deep, buried burned my hand on a hot sweet sewing needle, why squeeze, finger princess, my grease, or other bodily fluids, is dispensed in small amounts as his wishes, a tube, come true, like her trees, not likely, living a lie, a dreamscape, toes on the beach, her blue waves, from way outer space.
SETI: Search for Extra Terrestrial Intelligence, the designation of a series of projects based mainly on attempts to detect artificial radio transmissions from outer space.
The signals, all around.
> ♫ Diddley, Diddley, Diddley, Diddley, Daddy
> ♫ Diddley, Diddley, Diddley, Diddley, Daddy.

2

She was more real than Minute Minnie Mouse Maid fresh squeezed orange juice, the real McCoy, real him in.
Her ghost said: as you lift my veil ye who dares to yen I must plunge and smother and plague your endless ring small finger without a stitch, old wounds, I wouldn't put it past him, past lives, dim past.
There was a judgment issued by the Congregation for the Doctrine of the

Faith in a document titled *Inter Insigniores* that basically stated that since chapel veils were not a matter of faith, it was no longer mandatory for a ghost to wear, anything, with the naked eye, dazzled, naked as a jaybird, I see stars.

Howard Carter said to Canarvan: dingo duck disco delivery Dorothy don't lick the tomb walls, your hungry lip-smacking tongue dripping with saliva will ignite the three-thousand-year-old bacteria.

She licked her lips.

Zip your lip.

Bite my lip.

A King Cobra ate Carter's canary-yellow canary

Therefore, she was as invisible in light in the naked dark you couldn't see nothin.

> Dangle dug dump dupa
> Do did did done don't donkey does
> Double diagnosis dig
> Dope drab drape dragon.

3

Carter translated the ancient curse: the angle of the dangle is equal to the heat of the meat.

We were getting a cheese pizza, cause it was Friday and you had to fast from meat, at Maria Roma's pizzeria, and a bird got in the place somehow, that's the way it goes, some will die, bad luck, a bird will eat his soul, the souls of the dead return each sprang with her passionate and restless flocks, migrate, where once the moon temple, disoriented incant:

> Dark, double, dazed, deep, Debbie
> Doddle, duz, dysentery
> Dipple, dark, daze, dippy
> Debbie, deep
> Destiny, Durango
> Dispensary, dogsledder.

Her ghost said: by turning him round and promiscuously playing with certain magic, words, excite her love turned her into a bird, Darter, Dartford Warbler Dickcissel, Dodo, Iynx nymph jinx cast a spell on his ghost, which caused him to fall into love, with his love, alone, which the consequences, and metamorphosis, his white plume, can't.
♪ B-bird's the word a-well a bird bird bird
♪ B-bird's the word a-well a don't you know 'bout the bird
♪ Well everybody's knows a-bout the bird a-well-a bird bird bird
♪ B-birds the word.

L

Than This and That and Then, Ghosty Ghoul Meander

Part 1

His ghost said: I guess, my sad memory sadly disturbed cemetery markers, St. Stan's, by Sugar Road, were vandalized, broken, the records are incomplete, lost, there was a fire, can't recall, slip.
They are difficult to interpret, disappearing and reappearing as often as she often did depend on the depths of his mediocre melancholia, does, and he changes like the wind, water, under the bridge, and the deep blue sea between.
Use a mirror across from his face to make clear his past lives in the Villa Maria lawn fate beer tent or behind School 10, Alexander Street, her breath titillating coyness, her Lilith eyes, bleachers, ♪ It was twenty years ago today, Sgt. Pepper taught the band to play.
Zyn zyn poz zyn with soft light around her face, with a candle, with a mirror, he was able to summon her, demon, commune, Lesovik, with a long, kiss, after Vincent's closed, last call for alcohol, zyn wy poz zyn.
Her ghost said: you're a cut waiting to happen.
Time ran out, time acid rain can cause figures to lose their features, fingers blur her, writing, corrosive, illegible, within an hour the egg shell shall disappear, and his Clorox white, ghost does not remember, like a sieve, redial all the lost things he lost, in the fire, the flood, in his daily boredom, when he was moved, and ziz boom ba, that's all she wrote.

2 In the Morning

I was on the graveyard shift, midnight to 8 AM, Dracula shift, where everything foreboding, and darkly cloudy shadows colored appear shapes as everything beautiful sweet before the radiant dawn, purple, fingers, needing, a transplant, an infusion, that instant, struck by lightning, snapshot, the light went on.
His interpretation became hilarious brain, rain, punchy, being up too long, goofy, car wacky.
Loading the trucks in the warehouse, the night shift asshole gang called

him Igor, cause I was Old Teddy's helper.
They called Teddy SOS, Sack of Shit.
SOS also means Same Old Shit.
I helped SOS do the SOS.
♪ Working on a forklift
♪ In the night shift.
Greasy Wally was just stupid, called him Wally Zero, Wally O, but a nice guy.
Waller smoked so much that he could talk with his cigarette logged into his top lip like his lip was prehensile, spooky weird.
Stan would say things like when Eddie the forklift operator would say: I can't fit this in here. Stan would say: That's what she said: I can't fit that in here.
Victor sent Igor out to steal a brain, which he dropped. Fuck! Like when Wally went to get the subs, but he forgot what to get so everyone got meatball subs. I wanted salami, not bo-log-na, as they speakit in the France, salami, salami, bologna.
Stan* said they put the abnormal brain into Greasy Wally, was probably too big, cut it in half, that's what she said.
In *The Mummy* (2001), using a pliers the embalmer pulled out Imhotep's tongue out of his mouth, cut it off.
Cat got your tongue?
SNAFU: Situation Normal All Fucked Up.
Best of both words.
Someone left a book of curses in the men's shitter.
Wally didn't have too much to say, lost my brain of thought, senior moment.

*Stan is a poet from Buffalo, New York. His latest book *Hump Once, Bounce Twice* was published by Hole in a Sock Press. He is available for readings.

3

His ghost said: in writing class, I told everybody that I was hung for grave robbing.
In his next poem his brain was inserted in the monster's metaphor.

In his ghost vision of a curved rainbow bridge of hands: closed for repair. His ghost said: I thought it would be hard, I was always an immigrant, but it was so soft and easy, I did not believe I could ever be master this, cop, g, j, k, ch, ♪ Goo goo, goo goo barabajagal, ♪ Goo goo g'joob, Goo Goo Dolls.

In my native tongue the ghost Host sits on the tip of my tongue, most of the old markers are grey sedimentary rock, a taste, formed by deposits of minerals, such as calcite, and organisms, white, round moon white, such as coral and shell echoes echoes, time, where the loose balloons congregate, comingle with socks, lost, the taste.

The stone you are left with memory, disorder, might be: sandstone, slate, or the softest softer stone such as limestone or white marble utilized, powder during the early stages to puff, make-up her face life-like make out, *A Clockwork Orange*, devotchka.

Stan said: soft stone, that's what she said, Mr. Softy.

His ghost said: craved with arthritic hands by hand, hand it off, a hot hand, a bird in the hand, his.

His ghost in his ghost reading chair, empty, where he read all the great books of all the world to hell in a handbasket, can't hardly remember what happened in *The Mayor of Casterbridge*, *Middlemarch*, *Pamela*, *The Red and the Black*, yesterday.

King Tut's curse stated: all who enter a poem with impurity shall forget, he forgot her eye color, she wore a mask, cat woman, he was Zorro, her ghost said: who was that masked man, she forgot, stocking over his head. His ghost could invent it and why not, he was the master of the run-on sentence, correct poems, red marks, lice, Eczema cursed: you will have no unity in composition, there will be no end, completion, LOL.

His ghost pen automatic composition spewed this incant: erode, round a shimmering sunburned moment, smoldering, unhealed, monument, untied shoelaces and leaves, fingers, and lace lake dripping reptile garden hose, see thought monster fountain, to shake lustrous sheen glimpses, of her photographed photocopies with sand in her white eyes, become nights pearls, black pearls in her slip, Olga, clouds over and ocean and ocean, over the weak point, like pulling the covers up, pants up, no end in sight, so he changed the names, cover his ass.

Movement 4

Her ghost said: I am drunk drinking, DUI, DWI, under the table, shitfaced.
From her long green lactating breasts all exits all exists, the goddess Diana a booby trapped water fountain, Ponce De Leon drank, he's smashed, after finding the fountain of the young he died in July, in 1521, every year, repeat, has been/have been, it's July, refrain (refrain).
A flat tire on the wheel of the year.
Igor went about digging up the bodies to entice ghoul writing, *Egyptian Book of the Dead*, *Tibetan Book of the Dead*, spells, voila:

Gabaka viz
The dark noise of witch's eyes
O wu wha wu
Wanabe boo bow O
Jestabee jeestabee
Coo-kack.

Igor hoped to have his brain transplanted into his new body, which would, therefore, repair his malformations, long shot, *Paris Review*.
When sedimentary rock is exposed to the weather it slowly erodes, basically a reversal of the process from which it was created, faded rose, diminishes into silence, erased in the new day, back to normal.
Body snatching is directly tied to the advancement in the study of anatomy, medicine, and poetry, most of all, out of body, rupture, ur ooooob oc wubutoe wz ez uuuz oba up voop, came shooting out, shout.
Grave robbers seek jewels and are too often disappointed, they curse: shit, put a curse on, try on for size, ooot uuuj ooQoo ouuo, or maybe this one ⊂ ♪ ± ● ☽ ▼ ♩ *(*Improvise a translation and this improvisation might continue on into the empty, cold night of memory for some considerable slice of time or at least until the mind becomes an empty pop can recycled at Tops Friendly Market).

Coda

The Invasion of the Body Snatchers was an American horror film released in 1956. The film plots an alien invasion where alien plant spores have fallen from space and grow into large seed pods, like milkweed pods, each one capable of reproducing a duplicate replacement copy of each human. Assimilated humans have no emotions and are called pod people. Most of the pods were poets. The film begins with a ranting Matt Bennell* in custody in a hospital emergency room where he is screaming (at this point scream a lot). The film ends with the quiet invasion very much under way. After seeing a transport truck bound for San Francisco and New York City filled with the poets, he frantically screams at the passing motorists: They're here already! You're next! You're next!

*Matt Bennell's poems have appeared in *Pill Jar*, *Fart Machine*, and *Fourth Strike*. His most recent chapbook *Collapsed Star of Wonder Star of Night* was published by Zip-A-Dee-Doo-Dah-Gun Press. He lives in Cheektowaga, New York.

Finale

♪ Twas on a Wednesday afternoon
♪ He mounted on his mower
♪ The lawn was long, the grass was tall
♪ His mower it was red
♪ O he sang to himself, and he sang for himself
♪ What the ghosts incanted in his head
♪ O he sang to himself in tiny drops
♪ O his sang to himself like gazers
♪ O he sang to himself, he sang for himself
♪ The best poet in America
♪ O he sang to himself, and he sang for himself
♪ Klaatu barada nikto
♪ O he sang to himself, and he sang to himself
♪ What the ghosts incanted in his head
♪ Cut the grass on Wednesday noontime
♪ He rode upon his tractor
♪ O just an actor on a lawn
♪ Just an actor on a tractor
♪ O he sang to himself, and he sang for himself
♪ Just an asshole on a tractor.

Culled from MICHAEL BASINSKI's ego sheets was the recent appearance of the monograph *Salvage* (2019). In 2018, he published *Opems*, which documents his solo exhibition of large scale visual, sound, and performance opems (yes, o p e m s) at the Burchfield Penney Art Center. His 2017 books were *Unexplained Noises*, *Lot Sa Nots O*, and with the artist Ginny O'Brien, *Combinings*. "Combination of the Two," an exhibition of O'Brien's and Basinski's cooperative visual works/poems occurred in 2019 at the Western New York Book Arts Collaborative. In modern times his works have, by some miracle, appeared in *Peach Mag*, *Dispatches from the Poetry Wars*, *Angry Old Man*, *Journal of Poetic Research*, *Volt*, *Jacket2*, and in *The Canary Island Connection—60 Contemporary American Poets*. Just outside of Buffalo, New York, Michael Basinski lives just a little past the airport.

www.ingramcontent.com/pod-product-compliance
Lightning Source LLC
Chambersburg PA
CBHW030157100526
44592CB00009B/322